Big Wisdom
{LITTLE BOOK}

1,001

PROVERBS, ADAGES, AND

PRECEPTS TO HELP YOU

LIVE A BETTER LIFE

W PUBLISHING GROUP
A Division of Thomas Nelson Publishers
Since 1798

www.wpublishinggroup.com

Published by W Publishing Group, a Division of Thomas
Nelson, Inc., P.O. Box 141000, Nashville, Tennessee, 37214.

W Publishing Group books may be purchased in bulk for educa-
tional, business, fundraising, or sales promotional use. For information, please email SpecialMarkets@ThomasNelson.com.

All Scripture quotations, unless otherwise indicated, are taken
from The Message (MSG), copyright © 1993. Used by permis-
sion of NavPress Publishing Group.

Editorial Staff: Shady Oaks Studio, Bedford, Texas 76022
Cover Design: Kirk DouPonce, DogEared Design.com

Library of Congress Cataloging-in-Publication Data

Big wisdom : little book / [compiled by] Jim Palmer.
   p. cm.
   Summary: "1,002 quotes by those considered to be the wisest
in history"—Provided by publisher.
ISBN 0-8499-0506-0 (tradepaper)
1. Conduct of life—Quotations, maxims, etc.   2. Wisdom—
Quotations, maxims, etc.   I. Palmer, Jim, 1964–
PN6084.C556B54   2005
082—dc22   2005000783

Printed in Peru

06 07 08 09 QW 9 8 7 6 5 4 3 2

Introduction

——— ✳ ———

Putting together a collection of some of the wisest advice throughout history can be a daunting task. It goes without saying that thousands of nuggets were left behind in the wake of our selections for this anthology of prudence. Some of these we chose simply because they'll bring a grin; others will strike a deep place within; most will simply provide practical and worthwhile instruction on how to do life right.

You will find lots of ways that this book can come in handy. You may be asked to deliver a speech, or perhaps you have a paper to write, or you're looking for a way to impress your dinner guests with your refined wit. On the bottom of an e-mail or in a card, many of these quotations could serve as a timely and encouraging word to a friend or someone you care about. You may even be inspired to pick up a few extra copies and give them to your friends and family who could use a good dose of wisdom.

It is only fitting that the introduction to a book of quotes would itself contain a quote, therefore making 1,002 of them in total. A famous quip cautions, "After all is said and done, more is said than done." Once you've made your way through these 350 pages (good luck!), what really matters is what you go and do. In other words, the torch of wisdom has now been placed in your hands; don't extinguish it by doing nothing (or by losing it under your bed).

You may merely muse these pages for leisure or follow their guidance for life. It's your decision. Choose well!

—The Publisher

I love quotations because it is a joy to find thoughts one might have, beautifully expressed with much authority by someone recognized wiser than myself.

—*Marlene Dietrich*

The wisdom of the wise,
and the experience of ages, may be
preserved by quotation.
—*Isaac D'Israeli*

Success is the ability to go
from one failure to another with
no loss of enthusiasm.
—*Sir Winston Churchill*

I have decided to stick with love.
Hate is too great a burden to bear.
—*Martin Luther King Jr.*

Reduce the complexity of life by
eliminating the needless wants of life,
and the labors of life reduce themselves.
—*Edwin Way Teale*

Small opportunities are often the
beginning of great enterprises.
—*Demosthenes*

Everyone thinks of changing
the world, but no one thinks of
changing himself.
—*Leo Tolstoy*

Laughter is an instant vacation.
—*Milton Berle*

Every once in a while,
take the scenic route.
—*H. Jackson Brown Jr.*

There is nothing like returning to a
place that remains unchanged to find
the ways in which you yourself
have altered.
—*Nelson Mandela*

The more you know,
the less you need to show.
—*Author Unknown*

A carelessly planned project
takes three times longer to
complete than expected;
a carefully planned project
will take only twice as long.
—*Author Unknown*

Life is measured by the
number of things you are alive to.
—*Maltbie D. Babcock*

Failure is the opportunity to begin
again more intelligently.
—*Henry Ford*

The most important thing in commu-
nication is to hear what isn't being said.
—*Peter Drucker*

I can do no great things,
only small things with great love.
—*Mother Teresa*

Fatherhood is pretending the present
you love most is soap-on-a-rope.
—*Bill Cosby*

After you've done your best to deal with
a situation, avoid speculating about
the outcome. Forget it and go on
to the next thing.
—*Author Unknown*

Everybody needs beauty as well as bread,
places to play in and pray in, where nature
may heal and give strength to the body.
—*John Muir*

Anything you have not used for a year,
you do not need to keep. Don't think, "But
I might need it later!" If you made it
through last year without it, throw it
away—or give it to the Salvation Army for
somebody who needs it worse than you do.
—*Elisabeth Elliot*

Praise loudly, blame softly.
—*Russian Proverb*

Nothing gives one person so much an
advantage over another as to remain
always cool and unruffled
under all circumstances.
—*Thomas Jefferson*

Do not make the mistake of thinking
that concerned people cannot change the
world; it is the only thing that ever has.
—*Margaret Mead*

Opportunity is missed by most people
because it is dressed in overalls and
looks like work.
—*Thomas Edison*

7

Careful planning puts you ahead
in the long run;
hurry and scurry puts you
further behind.
—*King Solomon, Proverbs 2:15*

Put duties aside at least an hour
before bed and perform soothing,
quiet activities that will help
you relax.
—*Dianne Hales*

A well-adjusted person is one who makes the same mistake twice without getting nervous.
—*Author Unknown*

You must do the thing you think you cannot do.
—*Eleanor Roosevelt*

It is a common experience that a problem difficult at night is resolved in the morning after the committee of sleep has worked on it.
—*John Steinbeck*

When you say, "I'm sorry," look the person in the eye.
—*Author Unknown*

The greatest things happen only when
you give others the credit.
—*John C. Maxwell*

Forgive all who have offended you,
not for them, but for yourself.
—*Harriet Nelson*

Never eat Chinese food in Oklahoma.
—*Bryan Miller*

All that is necessary for the triumph of
evil is for good men to do nothing.
—*Edmund Burke*

We often dream of the splendors of
faraway places, but on introspection
those attractions are seldom as
precious as home.
—*Laura E. Richards*

I never look at the masses as my
responsibility. I look only at the
individual. I can love only one person at
a time. I can feed only one person at a
time. Just one, one, one.
—*Mother Teresa*

The best of my education has come
from the public library.
—*Lesley Conger*

Warning: Dates in calendar are
closer than they appear.
—*Author Unknown*

The fear of the Lord is the
beginning of knowledge,
but the end of knowledge is the
courage to act.
—*John Eldredge*

Watch for big problems; they disguise
big opportunities.
—*Author Unknown*

The way to love anything is to realize
that it may be lost.
—*G. K. Chesterton*

Be willing to be a beginner
every single morning.
—*Meister Eckhart*

The Bible is the one Book to which any
thoughtful man may go with any honest
question of life or destiny and find the
answer of God by honest searching.
—*John Ruskin*

Rome was not built in a day.
—*Latin Proverb*

You are never too old to set another
goal or to dream a new dream.
—*C. S. Lewis*

Drinking our cup is a hopeful,
courageous, and self-confident way of
living. It is standing in the world with
head erect, solidly rooted in the knowledge of who we are, facing the reality
that surrounds us and responding to it
from our hearts.
—*Henri Nouwen*

Pseudocommunity is conflict-avoiding;
true community is conflict-resolving.
—*M. Scott Peck*

Words kill, words give life;
they're either poison or fruit—
you choose.
—*King Solomon, Book of Proverbs*

Ducharm's Axiom: If you view your
problem closely enough, you will recognize yourself as part of the problem.
—*Author Unknown*

The least initial deviation from the
truth is multiplied later a thousandfold.
—*Aristotle*

When you realize you've made
a mistake, make amends
immediately. It's easier to eat
crow while it's still warm.
—*Dan Heist*

You will never plough a field if
you only turn it over in your mind.
—*Irish Proverb*

What is the use of spending one's time in continuous reading, turning the pages of the lives and sayings of holy men, unless we can extract nourishment from them by chewing and digesting this food so that its strength can pass into our inmost heart?
—*Guigo II the Carthusian Monk*

Jumping at several small opportunities may get us there more quickly than waiting for the big one to come along.
—*Sir Hugh Allen*

You will never find time for anything. If you want time you must make it.
—*Charles Buxton*

Do what you can, with what you have,
where you are.
—*Theodore Roosevelt*

Parents, don't come down too hard on
your children or you'll crush their spirits.
—*St. Paul, Colossians 3:21*

Finagle's Fourth Law: Once a job is
fouled up, anything done to improve it
only makes it worse.
—*Author Unknown*

Vitality shows not only in the ability to
persist, but in the ability to start over.
—*F. Scott Fitzgerald*

To consider persons and events and
situations only in the light of their effect
upon myself is to live on the
doorstep of hell.
—*Thomas Merton*

One of the true tests of leadership is
the ability to recognize a problem
before it becomes an emergency.
—*Arnold H. Glasgow*

One of the secrets of a long and fruit-
ful life is to forgive everybody, everything, every night before you go to bed.
—*Bernard M. Baruch*

To love what you do
and feel that it matters—
how could anything be more fun?
—*Katherine Graham*

Don't allow yourself to think
about the difficulties of step
number two until you've
executed step number one.
—*Author Unknown*

Adopt the pace of nature:
her secret is patience.
—*Ralph Waldo Emerson*

How far that little candle throws his
beams! So shines a good deed in a
weary world.
—*William Shakespeare*

Be ashamed to die until you have won
some great victory for humanity.
—*Horace Mann*

You can make more friends in two
months by becoming interested in other
people than you can in two years by trying to get other people interested in you.
—*Dale Carnegie*

Are you tired? Worn out? Burned out
on religion? Come to me. Get away
with me and you'll recover your life.
—*Jesus, Matthew 11:28*

Submission is the ability to lay down
the terrible burden of always needing
to get your own way.
—*Richard Foster*

Friendship redoubleth joys,
and cutteth griefs in half.
—*Francis Bacon*

You can't live a perfect day without
doing something for someone else who
will never be able to repay you.
—*John Wooden*

A bell is no bell 'til you ring it,
A song is no song 'til you sing it,
And love in your heart
wasn't put there to stay—
Love isn't love
'til you give it away.
—*Oscar Hammerstein,*
"Sixteen Going on Seventeen"

Do not look where you fell,
but where you stumbled.
—*African Proverb*

Wethern's Law: Assumption
is the mother of all screw-ups.
—*Author Unknown*

Happiness is neither within us only,
or without us; it is the union
of ourselves with God.
—*Blaise Pascal*

Just do it.
—*Nike Commercial*

In one of your braver moments,
ask your spouse for three things you
could improve on.
—*H. Norman Wright*

Every journey begins with a single step
and moves along one step at a time.
Enjoy the trip!
—*Ken Blanchard*

When you have to make a choice and
don't make it, that is in itself a choice.
—*William James*

May you live all the days of your life.
—*Jonathan Swift*

Lie #1: I must be perfect.
—*Chris Thurman*

The smallest deed is better than the
grandest intention.
—*Larry Eisenberg*

If you do not wish a man to do a thing,
you had better get him to talk about it;
for the more men talk, the more likely
they are to do nothing else.
—*Thomas Carlyle*

There are fine things which you mean to do some day, under what you think will be more favorable circumstances. But the only time that is surely yours is the present, hence this is the time to speak the word of appreciation and sympathy, to do the generous deed, to forgive the fault of a thoughtless friend, to sacrifice self a little more for others. Today is the day in which to express your noblest qualities of mind and heart, to do at least one worthy thing which you have long postponed, and to use your God-given abilities for the enrichment of someone less fortunate. Today you can make your life—significant and worthwhile. The present is yours to do with as you will.

—Grenville Kleiser

Take the first step in faith. You don't
have to see the whole staircase,
just take the first step.
—*Martin Luther King Jr.*

Defeat may serve as well as victory to
shake the soul and let the glory out.
—*Edwin Markham*

The art of living lies less in eliminating
our troubles than in growing with them.
—*Bernard M. Baruch*

You may not realize it when it happens, but a kick in the teeth may be the
best thing in the world for you.
—*Walt Disney*

Many of life's failures are people who
did not realize how close they were to
success when they gave up.
—*Thomas Edison*

Having two ears and one tongue,
we should listen twice as much
as we speak.
—*Turkish Proverb*

I think the next best thing to solving a
problem is finding some humor in it.
—*Frank A. Clark*

Be engaged at least six months
before you get married.
—*Author Unknown*

If I find in myself a desire which no
experience in this world can satisfy, the
most probable explanation is that I was
made for another world.
—*C. S. Lewis*

I took the road less traveled by,
and that has made all the difference.
—*Robert Frost*

O, begin! Fix some part of every
day for private exercises. . . .
Whether you like it or no, read
and pray daily. It is for your life;
there is no other way: else you will
be a trifler all your days. . . . Do
justice to your own soul; give it
time and means to grow. Do not
starve yourself any longer.
—*John Wesley*

Experience is not what happens
to you; it is what you do
with what happens to you.
—*Aldous Huxley*

The probability that we may fail in the
struggle ought not to deter us from the
support of a cause we believe to be just.
—*Abraham Lincoln*

It isn't that they can't see the solution.
It's that they can't see the problem.
—*G. K. Chesterton*

Humility means the eagerness to learn,
to keep growing, the willingness to
receive and be helped by the love and
gifts of others.
—*Flora Wuellner*

The art of progress is to preserve order
amid change, and to preserve change
amid order.
　　—*Alfred North Whitehead*

Take calculated risks. This is quite
different from being rash.
　　—*George S. Patton*

To buy books would be a good thing if
we also could buy the time to read
them. As it is, the act of purchasing
them is often mistaken for the assimila-
tion and mastering of their content.
　　—*Arthur Schopenhauer*

Speak when you are angry and you will
make the best speech
you will ever regret.
—*Ambrose Bierce*

We thought that we had the answers,
it was the questions we had wrong.
—*Bono*

Friends, this world is not your home,
so don't make yourselves too cozy in it.
Don't indulge your ego at the
expense of your soul.
—*St. Peter, 1 Peter 2:11*

The bars of life at which we fret,
That seem to prison and control,
Are but the doors of daring, set
Ajar before the soul.
—*Henry van Dyke*

Eighty percent of success is
showing up.
—*Woody Allen*

There is nothing which
God cannot effect.
—*Cicero*

One individual life may be of priceless
value to God's purposes, and yours
may be that life.
—*Oswald Chambers*

What good would it do to get everything you want and lose you, the real
you? What could you ever trade
your soul for?
—*Jesus, Mark 8:36–37*

I am profitably engaged in reading the
Bible. Take all of this Book upon reason
that you can and the balance upon
faith, and you will live and die a
better man.
—*Abraham Lincoln*

In order to console, there is no need to
say much. It is enough to listen, to
understand, to love.
—*Paul Tournier*

Even the saddest things can become,
once we have made peace with them, a
source of wisdom and strength for the
journey that still lies ahead.
—*Frederick Buechner*

Be like the turtle . . . if it didn't stick its
neck out, it wouldn't get anywhere
at all.
—*Harvey Mackay*

To me, old age is always fifteen years
older than I am.
—*Bernard M. Baruch*

Everyone wants to win on Saturday
afternoon when the game is played. It's
what you do the other six days that
decides the outcome.
—*Lou Holtz*

You've got to get to the stage of life where going for it is more important than winning or losing.
—*Arthur Ashe*

Parents wonder why the streams are bitter, when they themselves have poisoned the fountain.
—*John Locke*

Big pay and little responsibility are circumstances seldom found together.
—*Napoleon Hill*

It is no use walking anywhere to preach unless our walking is our preaching.
—*Saint Francis of Assisi*

Painful as it may be, a significant emotional event can be the catalyst for choosing a direction that serves us—and those around us—more effectively. Look for the learning.
—*Louisa May Alcott*

Do you wish to rise? Begin by descending. You plan a tower that will pierce the clouds? Lay first the foundation of humility.
—*Saint Augustine*

I find I am shedding hypocrisy in human relationships. What a rest that will be. The most exhausting thing in life, I have discovered, is being insecure.
—*Anne Morrow Lindbergh*

Those things that hurt instruct.
—*Benjamin Franklin*

Big Wisdom
{ LITTLE BOOK }

Silence is a text easy to misread.
—*A. A. Attanasio*

This above all: to thine own self be true,
And it must follow, as the night the day,
Thou canst not then be false to any man.
—*William Shakespeare*

Sow an act, reap a habit,
sow a habit, reap a character,
sow a character, reap a destiny.
—*Thomas à Kempis*

It is not what people eat, but what they digest, that makes them strong. It is not what they gain, but what they save, that makes them rich. It is not what they read, but what they remember, that makes them learned.
—*Henry Ward Beecher*

There's romance enough at home, without going half-a-mile for it; only people never think of it.
—*Charles Dickens*

I have found that being honest is the best technique I can use. Right up front, tell people what you're trying to accomplish and what you're willing to sacrifice to accomplish it.
—*Lee Iacocca*

It is well we should recognize that the business of education is with us all our lives, that we must always go on increasing our knowledge.
—*Charlotte Mason*

If you want to innovate, to change an enterprise or a society, it takes people willing to do what's not expected.
—*Jean Riboud*

A knowledge of the path cannot be
substituted for putting one foot
in front of the other.
—*M. C. Richards*

Lie # 2: I must have everyone's love
and approval.
—*Chris Thurman*

We need other people who will call
forth what is most beautiful in us, just as
we need to call forth what is most
beautiful in others.
—*Jean Vanier*

Fifteen minutes a day devoted to one
definite study will make one a master in
a dozen years.
—*Edward Howard Griggs*

The most important thing a father can
do for his children is to love their mother.
—*Theodore M. Hesburgh*

What a wonderful life I've had!
I only wish I'd realized it sooner.
—*Sidonie Gabrielle Colette*

The older I grow, the more I listen
to people who don't say much.
—*Germain G. Glidden*

Don't ever slam a door;
you might want to go back.
—*Don Herold*

God has not called me to be
successful. He has called me
to be faithful.
—*Mother Teresa*

There's a way that looks harmless
enough; look again.
—*King Solomon, Proverbs 16:2*

I cannot give you the formula for
success, but I can give you the formula
for failure—which is:
try to please everybody.
—*Herbert Bayard Swope*

No one is useless in this world who
lightens the burden of another.
—*Charles Dickens*

I am only one, but still I am one.
I cannot do everything,
but still I can do something;
And because I cannot do everything
I will not refuse to do the something
that I can do.
—*Edward Everett Hale*

If a man has a talent and cannot use it,
he has failed. If he has a talent and uses
only half of it, he has partly failed. If he
has a talent and learns somehow to use
the whole of it, he has gloriously
succeeded, and won a satisfaction and a
triumph few men know.
—*Thomas Wolfe*

I have learned to use the word
"impossible" with the greatest caution.
—*Wernher von Braun*

If you really want something, and really work hard, and take advantage of
opportunities, and never give up,
you will find a way.
—*Jane Goodall*

Bad will be the day for every man
when he becomes absolutely con-
tented with the life he is living,
with the thoughts that he is thinking, with the deeds he is doing,
when there is not forever beating
at the doors of his soul some
desire to do something larger,
which he knows that he was meant
and made to do because he is still,
in spite of all, the child of God.
—*Phillips Brooks*

It is never too late to give up
your prejudices.
—*Henry David Thoreau*

The bravest sight in all the world is a
man fighting against odds.
—*Franklin K. Lane*

If you always do what you always did,
you'll always get what you always got.
—*Author Unknown*

Do the thing you fear most and the
death of fear is certain.
—*Mark Twain*

God never gave man a thing to do
concerning which it were irreverent to
ponder how the Son of God
would have done it.
—*George Macdonald*

It would do the world good if every
man in it would compel himself occasionally to be absolutely alone. Most of
the world's progress has come out of
such loneliness.
—*Bruce Barton*

Not the power to remember, but its
very opposite, the power to forget, is a
necessary condition for our existence.
—*Saint Basil*

When one door closes another door
opens; but we so often look so long
and so regretfully upon the closed door,
that we do not see the ones
which open for us.
—*Alexander Graham Bell*

Leadership is the capacity to
translate vision into reality.
—*Warren G. Bennis*

Some of the greatest battles will be
fought within the silent chambers of
your own soul.
—*Ezra Taft Benson*

Life consists not in holding
good cards but in playing those
you hold well.
—*Josh Billings*

Push yourself again and again.
Don't give an inch until the final
buzzer sounds.
—*Larry Bird*

Show me a guy who's afraid to
look bad, and I'll show you a guy
you can beat every time.
—*Lou Brock*

If you compare yourself with others,
you may become vain and bitter, for
always there will be greater and lesser
persons than yourself.
—*Max Ehrmann*

Never lose sight of the fact that the
most important yardstick of your
success will be how you treat other
people—your family, friends, and
coworkers, and even strangers you
meet along the way.
—*Barbara Bush*

No one rises so high as he who knows
not whither he is going. Not only strike
while the iron is hot, but make it hot by
striking. Do not trust the cheering, for
those persons would shout as much if
you or I were going to be hanged.
—*Oliver Cromwell*

In seeking truth you have to get
both sides of a story.
—*Walter Cronkite*

Do exactly what you would do if you
felt most secure.
—*Meister Eckhart*

Might, could, would—they are
contemptible auxiliaries.
—*George Eliot*

The greatest challenge of the day is:
how to bring about a revolution of the
heart, a revolution which has to start
with each one of us.
—*Dorothy Day*

The man who removes a mountain
begins by carrying away small stones.
—*William Faulkner*

There can be no real freedom without
the freedom to fail.
—*Erich Fromm*

Be good at "letting go."
—*Marsha Sinetar*

Fulfillment comes from
developing your own talents, not
wishing for someone else's.
—*Author Unknown*

Whatever has been, has been and is finished. What is to be is yours now to choose. Now is the moment that you can influence. Now is the time to take positive action.
—*Ralph Marston*

The best remedy for those who are afraid, lonely, or unhappy is to go outside, somewhere were they can be quiet, alone with the heavens, nature, and God. Because only then does one feel that all is as it should be.
—*Anne Frank*

You must play boldly to win.
—*Arnold Palmer*

Between stimulus and response there is a space. In that space is our power to choose our response. In our response lies our growth and our freedom.
—*Viktor Frankl*

Your most unhappy customers are your greatest source of learning.
—*Bill Gates*

Being a Christian is more than just an instantaneous conversion; it is like a daily process whereby you grow to be more and more like Christ.
—*Billy Graham*

Big Wisdom
{ LITTLE BOOK }
——— ✳ ———

You miss 100 percent of the
shots you never take.
—*Wayne Gretzky*

He has the deed half done who has
made a beginning.
—*Horace*

All the forces in the world
are not so powerful as an idea
whose time has come.
—*Victor Hugo*

No man for any considerable period can
wear one face to himself and another to
the multitude, without finally getting
bewildered as to which may be the true.
—*Nathaniel Hawthorne*

He does not believe that does not
live according to his belief.
—*Thomas Fuller*

A single line in the Bible has con-
soled me more than all the books I
ever read besides.
—*Immanuel Kant*

No man can follow Christ
and go astray.
—*William H.P. Faunce*

God has given us two hands—one to
receive with and the other to give with.
We are not cisterns made for hoarding;
we are channels made for sharing.
—*Billy Graham*

Don't fret or worry. Instead of
worrying, pray. Let petitions and praises
shape your worries into prayers, letting
God know your concerns.
—*Saint Paul, Philippians 4:6*

God enters by a private door into
every individual.
—*Ralph Waldo Emerson*

He who leaves God out of his
reasoning does not know how to count.
—*Italian Proverb*

Do all the good you can,
By all the means you can,
In all the ways you can,
At all the times you can,
To all the people you can,
As long as ever you can.
—*John Wesley*

If I could live my life again, I'd spend more time playing with my children and grandchildren, less time watching professional athletes perform. More time enjoying what I have, less time thinking about the things I don't have.
—*Author Unknown*

Four things come not back: the spoken word; the sped arrows; time past; the neglected opportunity.
—*Horace*

The study of God's word, for the purpose of discovering God's will, is the secret discipline which has formed the greatest characters.
—*James W. Alexander*

The strength and the happiness
of a man consists in finding out
the way in which God is going,
and going in that way too.
—*Henry Ward Beecher*

He who provides for this life, but
takes no care for eternity, is wise
for a moment, but a fool forever.
—*John Tillotson*

The friend I need is one who confirms me, confronts me, and celebrates me.
—*James Nelson*

The learner always begins by finding fault, but the scholar sees the positive merit in everything.
—*Georg Hegel*

Nothing will ever be attempted if all possible objections must first be overcome.
—*Samuel Johnson*

Any man worth his salt will stick up for what he believes right, but it takes a slightly better man to acknowledge instantly and without reservation that he is in error.

—*Andrew Jackson*

The greatest accomplishment is not in never falling, but in rising again after you fall.

—*Vince Lombardi*

It is unlikely that we will deepen our relationship with God in a casual or haphazard manner. There will be a need for some intentional commitment and some reorganization in our own lives. But there is nothing that will enrich our lives more than a deeper and clearer perception of God's presence in the routine of daily living.

—*William O. Paulsell*

So never lose an opportunity of urging a practical beginning, however small, for it is wonderful how often in such matters the mustard-seed germinates and roots itself.

—*Florence Nightingale*

Leave no stone unturned.
—*Euripides*

Resolve never to quit,
never to give up, no matter
what the situation.
—*Jack Nicklaus*

Surround yourself with the best people
you can find, delegate authority, and
don't interfere as long as the
policy you've decided upon is
being carried out.
—*Ronald Reagan*

Getting close enough to see, hear,
touch, and taste the reality of others is
what always makes the difference.
—*Jim Wallis*

The smallest good act today is the
capture of a strategic point from which,
a few months later, you may be able to
go on to victories you never dreamed of.
—*C. S. Lewis*

A man should hear a little music, read
a little poetry, and see a fine picture
every day of his life, in order that
worldly cares may not obliterate the
sense of the beautiful which God has
implanted in the human soul.

—*Johann Wolfgang von Goethe*

The most powerful agent of growth
and transformation is something much
more basic than any technique:
a change of heart.

—*John Welwood*

Your heart is free,
have the courage to follow it.

—Malcolm Wallace, in *Braveheart*

What would you attempt to do if you
knew you would not fail?
—*Robert Schuller*

The only way to have a friend
is to be one.
—*Ralph Waldo Emerson*

The bitterest tears shed over graves are
for words left unsaid and deeds
left undone.
—*Harriet Beecher Stowe*

Journal writing is a voyage to
the interior.
—*Christina Baldwin*

He is no fool who gives that
which he cannot keep to gain
what he cannot lose.
—*Jim Elliot*

Wisdom is knowing what to do
next; virtue is doing it.
—*David Starr Jordan*

Great opportunities to help others
seldom come, but small ones
surround us daily.
—*Sally Koch*

The royal road to a man's heart is to
talk to him about the things he
treasures most.
—*Dale Carnegie*

To know the road ahead,
ask those coming back.
—*Chinese Proverb*

You learn more at a funeral than at a feast—after all, that's where we'll end up. We might discover something for it.
—*King Solomon, Ecclesiastes 7:2*

The unique ability to take decisive action while maintaining focus on the ultimate mission is what defines a true leader.
—*Robert Kiyosaki*

To find the universal elements enough; to find the air and the water exhilarating; to be refreshed by a morning walk or an evening saunter . . . to be thrilled by the stars at night; to be elated over a bird's nest or a wildflower in spring—these are some of the rewards of the simple life.
—*John Burroughs*

Despair at our imperfections is a
greater obstacle than the
imperfection itself.
—*François Fénelon*

Often the most helpful people have
endured suffering themselves and
turned their pain into a motivation to
serve others.
—*Gerald Sittser*

Anyone who proposes to do good must
not expect people to roll stones out of
his way, but must accept his lot calmly,
even if they roll a few stones upon it.
—*Albert Schweitzer*

The first duty of love is to listen.
—*Paul Tillich*

Our ultimate freedom is the
right and power to decide how
anybody or anything outside
ourselves will affect us.
—*Stephen Covey*

Care more than others think wise.
Risk more than others think safe.
Dream more than others think practical.
Expect more than others think possible.
—*Howard Schultz*

Every now and then go away, have a
little relaxation, for when you come
back to your work your judgment will
be surer; since to remain constantly at
work will cause you to lose your power
of judgment. Go some distance away
because the work appears smaller and
more of it can be taken in at a glance,
and a lack of harmony or proportion is
more readily seen.
—*Leonardo da Vinci*

You cannot teach people anything.
You can only help them discover it
within themselves.
—*Galileo*

We must be broken into life.
—*Charles E. Raven*

Never let the odds keep you from
pursuing what you know in your heart
you were meant to do.
—*Satchel Paige*

Not everything that is faced can be
changed, but nothing can be changed
until it is faced.
—*James A. Baldwin*

When you get into a tight place and
everything goes against you, till it seems
as though you could not hang on a
minute longer, never give up then,
for that is just the place and time
that the tide will turn.
—*Harriet Beecher Stowe*

Anger is an acid that can do more
harm to the vessel in which it is stored
than to anything on which it is poured.
—*Mark Twain*

Do not let what you cannot do interfere with what you can do.
—*John Wooden*

As I grow older, I pay less attention to what men say. I just watch what they do.
—*Andrew Carnegie*

True listening, total concentration on the other, is always a manifestation of love.
—*M. Scott Peck*

Self-pity is a deadly thing with the
power to destroy you.
—*Elisabeth Elliot*

No matter what you've done for yourself or for humanity, if you can't look
back on having given love and attention
to your own family, what have you
really accomplished?
—*Lee Iacocca*

The beginning of love is to let those we
love be perfectly themselves, and not to
twist them to fit our own image.
Otherwise we love only the reflection of
ourselves we find in them.
—*Thomas Merton*

In absence of clearly defined goals, we
become strangely loyal to performing
daily acts of trivia.
—*Author Unknown*

A hunch is creativity trying to
tell you something.
—*Frank Capra*

Do more than exist, live.
Do more than touch, feel.
Do more than look, observe.
Do more than read, absorb.
Do more than hear, listen.
Do more than listen, understand.
Do more than think, ponder.
Do more than talk, say something.
—*John H. Rhoades*

Lie # 3: It is easier to avoid problems
than to face them.
—*Chris Thurman*

Growing up means never having to say
you're perfect.
—*Peter Gzowski*

The conventional view serves to pro-
tect us from the painful job of thinking.
—*John Kenneth Galbraith*

It is easier to behave your way into a
new way of thinking than to think your
way into a new way of behaving.
—*Author Unknown*

People are unreasonable, illogical, and self-centered. Love them anyway. If you are kind, people may accuse you of selfish ulterior motives. Be kind anyway. If you are successful, you will win some false friends and true enemies. Succeed anyway. The good you do today will be forgotten tomorrow. Be good anyway. Honesty and frankness will make you vulnerable. Be honest and frank anyway. What you spend years building may be destroyed overnight. Build anyway. People need help but may attack you if you try to help them. Help them anyway. In the final analysis, it is between you and God. It was never between you and them anyway.

—Sign on the wall of a children's home in Calcutta

The problem of choosing to love again
is that the choice to love means living
under the constant threat of further loss.
But the problem of choosing not to love
is that the choice to turn from love means
imperiling the life of the soul, for the soul
thrives in an environment of love.
—*Gerald Sittser*

It is our duty as men and women to
proceed as though the limits of our
abilities do not exist.
—*Pierre Teilhard de Chardin*

He is a wise man who does not grieve
for the things which he has not, but
rejoices for those which he has.
—*Epictetus*

I attribute the little I know to my not having been ashamed to ask for information, and to my rule of conversing with all descriptions of men on those topics that form their own peculiar professions and pursuits.

—*John Locke*

One person with a belief is equal to ninety-nine who have only interests.

—*John Stuart Mill*

We do not have all the flexibility in
our lives to be able to make the time
and establish the space for a weekly day
of apartness. But, let's be realistic here.
There is in the lives of most of us a
good bit more freedom and flexibility to
organize such a dimension,
if we really want to.
—*Basil Pennington*

I believe we would be happier to have a personal revolution in our individual lives and go back to simpler living and more direct thinking. It is the simple things of life that make living worthwhile, the sweet fundamental things such as love and duty, work and rest, and living close to nature. There are not hothouse blossoms that can compare in beauty and fragrance with my bouquet of wildflowers.

—*Laura Ingalls Wilder*

Big Wisdom
{ LITTLE BOOK }
——— ✳ ———

Finding out who we really are and
what we truly want is perhaps best discovered by learning about others who
are in the process of doing the same.
—*Linda Breen Pierce*

Children are no casual guests in our
home. They have been loaned to us
temporarily for the purpose of loving
them and instilling a foundation of
values on which their future lives
will be built.
—*James Dobson*

Y ou know that the beginning is the most important part of any work, especially in the case of a young and tender thing; for that is the time at which the character is being formed and the desired impression is more readily taken.

—*Plato*

W e should also take notice of the errors into which we naturally tend to fall. Having discovered our errors, we must force ourselves off in the opposite direction.

—*Aristotle*

If I can stop one heart from breaking,
I shall not live in vain;
If I can ease one life the aching,
Or cool one pain,
Or help one fainting robin
Unto his nest again,
I shall not live in vain.
—*Emily Dickinson*

Tell the truth at all times and in all
places. It is better to have a reputation
for truthfulness than one for wit,
wisdom, or brilliance.
—*Nineteenth-century book,*
Correct Manners,
a Complete Handbook of Etiquette

To keep myself physically strong,
mentally awake, and
morally straight.
—*From the Boy Scout Oath*

Things not to worry about:
Don't worry about popular opinion.
—*F. Scott Fitzgerald*

We shall do much
in the years to come,
But what have we done today?
We shall give our gold
in a princely sum,
But what did we give today?
We shall lift the heart and dry the tear,
We shall plant a hope in the
place of fear,
We shall speak the words of love and cheer,
But what did you speak today?
—*Nixon Waterman*

We are, in truth, more than half what we are, by imitation. The great point is, to choose good models, and study them with care. Persist, therefore, in keeping the best company, and you will sensibly become like them.

—*Lord Chesterfield*

Little things are often our hardest tests. Out of pride, we are apt to overlook these little things, because they are so small.

—*John Bunyan*

Do whatever it takes. Remember, there
is very little traffic in the extra mile.
—*Kevin Freiberg*

Your problem is to bridge the gap
which exists between where you are now
and the goal you intend to reach.
—*Earl Nightingale*

Are you conceivably that man or
woman in your own sphere of influence
on whom God has placed his finger and
said, "This is your time, your cause,
your calling?"
—*J. Douglas Holladay*

Our lives begin to end the day we
become silent about things
that matter.
—*Martin Luther King Jr.*

Most of us know perfectly well
what we ought to do; our trouble is
that we do not want to do it.
—*Peter Marshall*

It is easy to love the people far away. It is not always easy to love those close to us. It is easier to give a cup of rice to relieve hunger than to relieve the loneliness and pain of someon · unloved in our own home. Bring love into your home for this is where our love for each other must start.

—*Mother Teresa*

It pays to know the enemy—not least because at some time you may have the opportunity to turn him into a friend.

—*Margaret Thatcher*

Nearly every man who develops an idea works it up to the point where it looks impossible, and then he gets discouraged. That's not the place to become discouraged.
—*Thomas Edison*

If you can dream it, you can do it. Always remember that this whole thing was started with a dream and a mouse.
—*Walt Disney*

Try to learn something about everything and everything about something.
—*Thomas H. Huxley*

Let me tell you the secret that has led
me to my goal. My strength lies
solely in my tenacity.
—*Louis Pasteur*

Each indecision brings its own delays
and days are lost lamenting over lost
days. . . . What you can do or think you
can do, begin it. For boldness has
magic, power, and genius in it.
—*Johann Wolfgang von Goethe*

Great leaders are almost always great
simplifiers, who can cut through
argument, debate, and doubt, to offer a
solution everybody can understand.
—*Colin Powell*

Justice is truth in action.
—*Benjamin Disraeli*

One man with courage
makes a majority.
—*Andrew Jackson*

The biggest mistake people make in
life is not trying to make a living at
doing what they most enjoy.
—*Malcolm S. Forbes*

Make every thought, every fact, that
comes into your mind pay you a profit.
Make it work and produce for you.
Think of things not as they are but as
they might be. Don't merely dream—
but create!
—*Robert Collier*

I think in terms of the day's resolutions,
not the years'.
—*Henry Moore*

You are remembered for
the rules you break.
—*Douglas MacArthur*

Never tell people how to do things.
Tell them what to do and they will
surprise you with their ingenuity.
—*George S. Patton*

When placed in command—
take charge.
—*Norman Schwarzkopf*

Few things can help an individual
more than to place responsibility
on him, and to let him know
that you trust him.
—*Booker T. Washington*

It is better to wear out than to rust out.
—*Richard Cumberland*

Example is not the main thing in influencing others. It is the only thing.
—*Albert Schweitzer*

Carry out a random act of kindness, with no expectation of reward, safe in the knowledge that one day someone might do the same for you.
—*Princess Diana*

Here is a simple, rule of thumb guide for behavior: Ask yourself what you want people to do for you, then grab the initiative and do it for them.
—*Jesus, Matthew 7:12*

Whatever you are by nature,
keep to it; never desert your line of
talent. Be what nature intended
you for, and you will succeed.
—*Sydney Smith*

Be not angry that you cannot
make others as you wish them to
be, since you cannot make yourself
as you wish to be.
—*Thomas à Kempis*

When a dream takes hold of you,
what can you do? You can run with it,
let it run your life, or let it go and think
for the rest of your life about what
might have been.
—*Patch Adams*

Learn to . . . be what you are, and
learn to resign with a good grace all that
you are not.
—*Henri Frederic Amiel*

Sometimes the best way to figure out
who you are is to get to that place where
you don't have to be anything else.
—*Author Unknown*

Don't fear change—embrace it.
—*Anthony J. D'Angelo*

There was that law of life, so cruel and
so just, that one must grow or else pay
more for remaining the same.
—*Norman Mailer*

Read, every day, something no one else
is reading. Think, every day, something
no one else is thinking. Do, every day,
something no one else would be silly
enough to do. It is bad for the mind to
continually be part of unanimity.
—*Christopher Morley*

You don't need a weatherman to know
which way the wind blows.
—*Bob Dylan*

Don't let life discourage you;
everyone who got where he is had to
begin where he was.
—*Richard L. Evans*

To dare to live alone is the rarest
courage; since there are many who
had rather meet their bitterest enemy
in the field, than their own hearts
in their closet.
—*Charles Caleb Colton*

He drew a circle that shut me out
Heretic, rebel, a thing to flout.
But love and I had the wit to win:
We drew a circle that took him in.
—*Edwin Markham*

Too often we underestimate the
power of a touch, a smile, a kind
word, a listening ear, an honest
compliment, or the smallest act of
caring, all of which have the
potential to turn a life around.
—*Leo Buscaglia*

Only as high as I reach can I grow,
Only as far as I seek can I go,
Only as deep as I look can I see,
Only as much as I dream can I be.
—*Karen Ravn*

Whatever you want to do, do it now.
There are only so many tomorrows.
—*Michael Landon*

Keep close to Jesus.
—*Paul the Great, Desert Father,*
Fourth Century

If you notice something evil in yourself,
correct it; if something good, take care
of it; if something beautiful, cherish it;
    if something sound, preserve it; if
somethig unhealthy, heal it. Do not
weary of reading the commandments
of the Lord, and you will be adequately
instructed by them so as to know what
    to avoid and what to go after.
    —*Bernard of Chartres, French Scholar,*
        Twelfth Century

Never listen to accounts of the frailties
of others and if anyone should com-
plain to you of another, humbly ask him
    not to speak of him at all.
    —*Saint John of the Cross*

Talk low, talk slow,
and don't say too much.
—*John Wayne*

Know that even when you are in the
kitchen, our Lord moves amidst the pots
and pans.
—*Teresa of Avila*

Be careful to preserve your health. It is
a trick of the devil, which he employs to
deceive good souls, to incite them to do
more than they are able, in order that
they may no longer be able
to do anything.
—*Vincent de Paul*

Nobody makes a greater mistake
than he who does nothing because
he could only do a little.
—*Edmund Burke*

Each day you must say to
yourself, "Today I am going
to begin."
—*Jean Pierre de Caussade*

There is nothing that makes us love a man so much as praying for him.
—*William Law*

And you will do well if you can prevail upon some intimate and judicious friend to be your constant hearer, and allow him with the utmost freedom to give you notice of whatever he shall find amiss.
—*Jonathan Swift*

To be like Christ is to be a Christian.
—*William Penn*

The tragedy of life is not so much what
men suffer, but rather what they miss.
—*Thomas Carlyle*

The silent power of a consistent life.
—*Florence Nightingale*

When God wants to do his great works
he trains somebody to be quiet enough
and little enough, then he uses
that person.
—*James Hudson Taylor*

None but God can satisfy the longings
of an immortal soul; that as the heart
was made for Him, so He only can fill it.
—*Richard Chevenix Trench*

Never make a principle out of your experience; let God be as original with other people as he is with you.
—*Oswald Chambers*

Never force religious instruction on your child. It is far more important for him to feel the impact of your faith. If you faith is really living in you, you will not need to depend on pious words: your children will sense it in your daily life and in your contact with them.
—*Johann Christoph Arnold*

Is prayer your steering wheel or your spare tire?
—*Corrie Ten Boom*

Never say that you have no time. On the whole it is those who are busiest who can make time for yet more, and those who have more leisure-time who refuse to do something when one asks. What we lack is not time, but heart.
—*Henri Boulard*

Make your one aim in life the doing of the will of Jesus in every circumstance, however important or trifling it may seem.
—*Ignatii Brianchaninov*

There are a lot of things that only happen once. Remembering that simple fact will help us live through them.
—*Jill Briscoe*

What God does first and best and most is to trust his people with their moment in history. He trusts them to do what must be done for the sake of his whole humanity.
—*Walter Brueggemann*

God wills to do something quite definite and particular through us, here and now, something which no other person could do at any other time.
—*Emil Brunner*

In the spiritual journey we travel through the night towards the day. We walk not in the bright sunshine of total certainty but through the darkness of ignorance, error, muddle, and uncertainty. We make progress in the journey as we grow in faith.
—*Christopher Bryant*

Suppose everybody cared enough, everybody shared enough, wouldn't everybody have enough? There is enough in the world for everyone's need, but not enough for everyone's greed.
—*Frank Buchman*

My secret is quite simple—I pray.
—*Mother Teresa*

There is something much greater than
human action—prayer.
—*Carlo Carretto*

When will we teach our children in
school what they are? We should say to
each of them: Do you know what you
are? You are a marvel . . . And when
you grow up, can you then harm another
who is, like you, a marvel?
—*Pablo Casals*

Spirituality is nothing less than
the whole of life oriented towards
God, shaped by God,
graced by God.
—*Jim Cotter*

No one has a right to sit down and
feel hopeless. There's too much
work to do.
—*Dorothy Day*

I believe it is of real value to our earthly life to have the next life in mind, because if we shut it out of our thoughts we are starving part of our spiritual nature—we are like children who fail to grow up—none the finer children for that.

—*Joan Mary Fry*

Our problem is not that we take refuge from action in spiritual things, but that we take refuge from spiritual things in action.

—*Monica Furlong*

We are not permitted to choose the frame of our destiny. But what we put into it is ours.

—*Dag Hammarskjöld*

Saying goodbye to a loved one is not the same as forgetting them or ceasing to think of them. It is simply the way of owning the loss, integrating it, accepting its restrictions and limitations and saying yes to life without the one who has died.

—*Joyce Huggett*

We should read to give our souls a
chance to luxuriate.
—*Henry Miller*

Do not walk through time without
leaving worthy evidence of
your passage.
—*Pope John XXIII*

If you wish to be fully alive you must
develop a sense of perspective. Life is
infinitely greater than this trifle your
heart is attached to and which you have
given the power to so upset you.
—*Anthony de Mello*

Outside show is a poor
substitute for inner worth.
—*Aesop*

No one can make you feel
inferior
without your consent.
—*Eleanor Roosevelt*

Do not always look for gratitude,
for sometimes when you are most
deserving, you will get the least.
—*Ida Scudder*

The real and important world is the
world inside us, not the world outside.
—*David Watson*

If a man insisted always on being
serious, and never allowed himself a bit
of fun and relaxation, he would go mad
or become unstable without knowing it.
—*Herodotus*

Love talked about can be easily turned
aside, but love demonstrated
is irresistible.
—*Stan Mooneyham*

Don't let a little dispute injure
a great friendship.
—*Author Unknown*

Become wise by walking with the wise;
hang out with fools and watch your life
fall to pieces.
—*King Solomon, Proverbs 13:20*

Let each man pass his days in that
wherein his skill is greatest.
—*Sextus Propertius*

Don't look for shortcuts to God. The market is flooded with surefire, easygoing formulas for a successful life that can be practiced in your spare time. Don't fall for that stuff, even though crowds of people do. The way to life— to God!—is vigorous and requires total attention.
—*Jesus, Matthew 7:13–14*

Keep to moderation, keep the end in view, follow nature.
—*Lucan*

To change your mind and to follow him who sets you right is to be nonetheless the free agent that you were before.
—*Marcus Aurelius Antoninus*

A great flame follows a
little spark.
—*Dante*

Be not angry that you cannot
make others as you wish them to
be, since you cannot make yourself
as you wish to be.
—*Thomas à Kempis*

Husbands, go all out in your love for
your wives, exactly as Christ did for the
church—a love marked by giving,
not getting.
—*Saint Paul, Ephesians 5:25*

The best mirror is an old friend.
—*George Herbert*

By speaking of our misfortunes we
often relieve them.
—*Pierre Corneille*

It is always darkest just before
the day dawneth.
—*Thomas Fuller*

In necessary things, unity; in doubtful
things, liberty; in all things, charity.
—*Richard Baxter*

Beware, as long as you live, of judging
people by appearances.
—*Jean de la Fontaine*

Do you wish people to think well of
you? Don't speak well of yourself.
—*Blaise Pascal*

New opinions are always suspected,
and usually opposed, without any other
reason but because they are not
already common.
—*John Locke*

Choose an author as you choose
a friend.
—*Wentworth Dillon*

No time like the present.
—*Mary de la Riviere Mantley*

To let friendship die away by
negligence and silence, is certainly
not wise. It is voluntarily to throw
away one of the greatest comforts
of this weary pilgrimage.
—*Samuel Johnson*

A goal is a dream
with a deadline.
—*Napoleon Hill*

My rule always was to do the business
of the day in the day.
—*Arthur Wellesley*

First say to yourself what you would be;
and then do what you have to do.
—*Epictetus*

We may affirm absolutely that nothing
great in the world has been
accomplished without passion.
—*Georg Hegel*

It is now almost my sole rule in life to
clear myself of cants and formulas.
—*Thomas Carlyle*

He is invited to do great things who
receives small things greatly.
—*Cassiodorus, Roman Monk, Sixth Century*

It's only human to want to make a buck,
but it's better to be poor than a liar.
—*King Solomon, Proverbs 19:22*

As Man alone, Jesus could not have
saved us; as God alone, he would not;
Incarnate, he could and did.
—*Malcolm Muggeridge*

If a man does not keep pace with his companions, perhaps it is because he hears a different drummer. Let him step to the music which he hears, however measured or far away.
—*Henry David Thoreau*

The hand that rocks the cradle
Is the hand that rules the world.
—*William Ross Wallace*

To own a bit of ground, to scratch it with a hoe, to plant seeds, and watch the renewal of life—this is the commonest delight of the race, the most satisfactory thing a man can do.
—*Charles Dudley Warner*

If you want a golden rule that will fit everybody, this is it: Have nothing in your houses that you do not know to be useful, or believe to be beautiful.
—*William Morris*

The secret of my success is that at an early age I discovered I was not God.
—*Oliver Wendell Holmes*

Minds are like parachutes. They only
function when they are open.
—*Sir James Dewar*

Anything that God has ever done, He
can do now. Anything that God has
done anywhere else, He can do here.
Anything that God has done for anyone
else, He can do for me.
—*Author Unknown*

But I predict that just when you see
with horror that in spite of all your
efforts you are getting further from your
goal instead of nearer to it—at that very
moment I predict that you will reach it
and behold clearly the miraculous
power of the Lord who has been
all the time loving and mysteriously
guiding you.
—*Fyodor Dostoyevsky*

Keep company with God,
get in on the best.
—*King David, Psalms 37:4*

Conceal a flaw, and the world will
imagine the worst.
—*Martial*

When we walk to the edge of all the light we have and take that step into the darkness of the unknown, we must believe that one of two things will happen . . . There will be something solid to stand on, or we will be taught to fly.
—*Author Unknown*

Make no little plans; they have no magic to stir men's blood.
—*Daniel Hudson Burnham*

A man travels the world over in search of what he needs and returns home to find it.
—*George Moore*

Y ou see things and you say, "Why?"
But I dream things that never were
and I say, "Why not?"
—*George Bernard Shaw*

T rust yourself.
You know more than you
think you do.
—*Benjamin Spock*

Let us never negotiate out of fear, but
let us never fear to negotiate.
—*John F. Kennedy*

You're either part of the solution or
part of the problem.
—*Eldridge Cleaver*

I expect to pass through this world but
once; any good thing therefore that I
can do, or any kindness that I can show
to any fellow creature, let me do it now,
let me not defer or neglect it, for I shall
not come this way again.
—*Author Unknown*

Never take the advice of someone who
has not had your kind of trouble.
—*Sidney J. Harris*

Walking is the best possible exercise.
Habituate yourself to walk very far.
—*Thomas Jefferson*

Eat breakfast like a king, lunch like a
prince, and dinner like a pauper.
—*Adelle Davis*

Patterning your life around other's
opinions is nothing more than slavery.
—*Lawana Blackwell*

Be courteous to all, but intimate with
few, and let those few be well tried
before you give them your confidence.
True friendship is a plant of slow
growth, and must undergo and with-
stand the shocks of adversity before it is
entitled to the appellation.
—*George Washington*

Call it a clan, call it a network, call it a
tribe, call it a family. Whatever you call
it, whoever you are, you need one.
—*Jane Howard*

I've always believed that a lot of the trouble in the world would disappear if we were talking to each other instead of about each other.
—*Ronald Reagan*

Fear is that little darkroom where negatives are developed.
—*Michael Pritchard*

The most important work you and I
will ever do will be within the walls of
our own homes.
—*Harold B. Lee*

When in doubt, tell the truth.
—*Mark Twain*

It was, of course, a grand and
impressive thing to do, to mistrust the
obvious, and to pin one's faith in things
which could not be seen.
—*Galen*

Good ideas are not adopted
automatically. They must be driven into
practice with courageous patience.
—*Hyman Rickover*

We should be taught not to wait for inspiration to start a thing. Action always generates inspiration. Inspiration seldom generates action.
—*Frank Tibolt*

Envy is the ulcer of the soul.
—*Socrates*

There is no greater joy nor greater reward than to make a fundamental difference in someone's life.
—*Sister Mary Rose McGready*

The dead cannot cry out for justice; it is a duty of the living to do so for them.
—*Lois McMaster Bujold*

The best thing to give to your enemy is
forgiveness; to an opponent, tolerance;
to a friend, your heart; to your child, a
good example; to a father, deference; to
your mother, conduct that will make her
proud of you; to yourself, respect;
to all men, charity.
—*Francis Maitland Balfour*

He who laughs, lasts!
—*Mary Pettibone Poole*

We can only learn to love by learning.
—*Iris Murdoch*

A good listener is not only
popular everywhere, but after a
while he gets to know something.
—*Wilson Mizner*

A successful marriage is an edi-
fice that must be rebuilt every day.
—*André Maurois*

To be mature means to face, and not
evade, every fresh crisis that comes.
—*Fritz Kunkel*

To avoid situations in which you might
make mistakes may be the biggest
mistake of all.
—*Peter McWilliams*

Obstacles don't have to stop you. If
you run into a wall, don't turn around
and give up. Figure out how to climb it,
go through it, or work around it.
—*Michael Jordan*

Risk! Risk everything! Care no more
for the opinions of others, for those
voices. Do the hardest thing on earth for
you. Act for yourself. Face the truth.
—*Katherine Mansfield*

Trouble is only opportunity in
work clothes.
—*Henry J. Kaiser*

The most important thing she'd
learned over the years was that there
was no way to be a perfect mother and
a million ways to be a good one.
—*Jim Churchill*

Waste no time talking about great
souls and how they should be.
Become one yourself.
—*Marcus Aurelius Antoninus*

Passion is the quickest to develop, and
the quickest to fade. Intimacy develops
more slowly, and commitment more
gradually still.
—*Robert Sternberg*

Have patience with all things, but
chiefly have patience with yourself. Do
not lose courage in considering your
own imperfections but instantly set
about remedying them—every day
begin the task anew.
—*Saint Francis de Sales*

First keep the peace within yourself, then you can also bring peace
to others.
—*Thomas à Kempis*

The thing that is really hard, and
really amazing, is giving up on
being perfect and beginning the
work of becoming yourself.
—*Anna Quindlen*

A model is someone who demonstrates
new ways of living in spite of all the
chaos, someone who remains loving and
humble in spite of all the violence,
someone who does not judge or condemn. Through their lives, these people
show us a bigger picture: that there is a
way to peace and unity, even though it
may involve struggle and pain.

—*Jean Vanier*

In all your deeds and words you should
look on Jesus as your model, whether
you are keeping silence or speaking,
whether you are alone or with others.

—*Bonaventure*

There is no freedom like seeing myself
as I am and not losing heart.
—*Macrina Wiederkehr*

Rules of the road: What appears to be
a detour may be the most important leg
of the journey.
—*Judy Cannato*

Easy come, easy go,
but steady diligence pays off.
—*King Solomon, Proverbs 13:11*

What to do in the darkness: go slowly;
consent to it, but don't wallow in it;
know it as a place of germination and
growth; remember the light; take an
outstretched hand if you find one;
exercise unused senses; find the path by
walking on it; practice trust;
watch for dawn.
—*Marilyn Chandler McEntyre*

Jones' Law: The man who smiles when
things go wrong has thought of someone to blame it on.
—*Author Unknown*

Never discourage anyone who
continually makes progress,
no matter how slow.
—*Plato*

There is no competition between
lighthouses. There's so much need
for good in this world, we'll never
have too many candles
or lighthouses.
—*M. Norvel Young*

Set up as an ideal the facing of reality
as honestly and cheerfully as possible.
—*Karl Menninger*

The real distinction is between those
who adapt their purposes to reality and
those who seek to shape reality in the
light of their purposes.
—*Henry Kissinger*

Blessed is the man who can love all
men equally.
—*Maximus the Confessor, Greek Theologian,
Seventh Century*

Take rest; a field that has rested gives a
bountiful crop.
—*Ovid*

You can't build a reputation on
what you are going to do.
—*Henry Ford*

Our lives improve when we take
chances—and the first and most
difficult risk we can take is to be honest
with ourselves.
—*Walter Anderson*

Insanity: doing the same thing over
and over again and expecting
different results.
—*Albert Einstein*

You're only given a little spark of
madness. You mustn't lose it.
—*Robin Williams*

There is a time for many words, and
there is also a time for sleep.
—*Homer*

Wherever you are, be all there.
—*Jim Elliot*

Whenever I hear, "It can't be done,"
I know I'm close to success.
—*Michael Flatley*

We can draw lessons from the past,
but we cannot live in it.
—*Lyndon B. Johnson*

Measure twice because
you can only cut once.
—*Author Unknown*

A friend who seeks to be a substitute for God is no friend! A true friend will point you to God and help you build a relationship with Him.
—*Charles Stanley*

Maturity:
Be able to stick with a job until it is finished. Be able to bear an injustice without having to get even. Be able to carry money without spending it. Do your duty without being supervised.
—*Ann Landers*

The truth that makes men free is for
the most part the truth which men
prefer not to hear.
—*Herbert Agar*

We improve ourselves by victories over
ourself. There must be contests,
and you must win.
—*Edward Gibbon*

One's first step in wisdom is to
question everything—and one's last is to
come to terms with everything.
—*Georg Lichtenberg*

No man is wise enough by himself.
—*Titus Maccius Plautus*

He who begins many things
finishes but a few.
—*Italian Proverb*

In order that people may be happy in
their work, these three things are
needed: They must be fit for it. They
must not do too much of it. And they
must have a sense of success in it.
—*John Ruskin*

What worries you masters you.
—*Haddon W. Robinson*

Leadership is getting someone to do
what they don't want to do in order to
achieve what they want to achieve.
—*Tom Landry*

This is your life,
are you who you want to be?
—*Jonathan Foreman*

When you recover or discover
something that nourishes your soul and
brings joy, care enough about yourself
to make room for it in your life.
—*Jean Bolen*

The greatest foes, and whom we must
chiefly combat, are within.
—*Miguel de Cervantes*

Be nice to people on your way up
because you might meet them on your
way down.
—*John Dryden*

Let us not be content to wait and
see what will happen, but give us
the determination to make the
right things happen.
—*Peter Marshall*

The best way out is always
through.
—*Robert Frost*

The trick is growing up
without growing old.
—*Casey Stengel*

I have never in my life learned anything
from any man who agreed with me.
—*Dudley Field Malone*

When two men in business always
agree, one of them is unnecessary.
—*William Wrigley Jr.*

Anger: an acid that can do more harm
to the vessel in which it is stored than to
anything on which it is poured.
—*Seneca*

If you fear making anyone mad, then
you ultimately probe for the lowest
common denominator of human
achievement.
—*Jimmy Carter*

Empty pockets never held anyone
back. Only empty heads and empty
hearts can do that.
—*Norman Vincent Peale*

The elevator to success is out of order.
You'll have to use the stairs . . . one step
at a time.
—*Joe Girard*

Good questions outrank easy answers.
—*Paul A. Samuelson*

Let no man undervalue the price of a
virtuous woman's counsel.
—*George Chapman*

The only pressure I'm under is the
pressure I've put on myself.
—*Mark Messier*

It's not how much we have, but how
much we enjoy, that makes happiness.
—*Charles Haddon Spurgeon*

He who angers you conquers you.
—*Elizabeth Kenny*

If you don't run your own life,
somebody else will.
—*John Atkinson*

He that won't be counseled
can't be helped.
—*Benjamin Franklin*

Wise men still seek Him today.
—*Dan Bell*

Once conform, once do what others
do because they do it, and a kind of
lethargy steals over all the finer senses
of the soul.
—*Montaigne*

Leave everything a little
better than you found it.
—*H. Jackson Brown Jr.*

Even if you are on the right track,
you'll get run over if you just sit there.
—*Will Rogers*

Why not upset the apple cart? If you
don't the apples will rot anyway.
—*Carl W. Buechner*

Caring is a powerful business
advantage.
—*Scott Johnson*

God does not desire "something" from
us—he desires us, ourselves; not our
works, but our personality, our will,
our hearts.
—*Emil Brunner*

Looking back, I have this one regret,
that too often when I loved,
I did not say so.
—*David Grayson*

A man can fail many times, but he isn't
a failure until he begins to blame
somebody else.
—*John Burroughs*

When you cannot make up your mind
which of two evenly balanced courses
of action you should take—choose
the bolder.
—*William Joseph Slim*

Reading is to the mind what exercise is
to the body.
—*Joseph Addison*

Reading is a basic tool in the living of
a good life.
—*Mortimer J. Adler*

You tend to be afraid when someone seems foreign to you. But if you aren't careful, that can lead to bigotry.
—*Jasmine Guy*

The most valuable of all talents is that of never using two words when one will do.
—*Thomas Jefferson*

Until you make peace with who you
are, you'll never be content
with what you have.
—*Doris Mortman*

A house without books is like a room
without windows.
—*Horace Mann*

No one can drive us crazy unless we
give them the keys.
—*Doug Horton*

Everything someone does on a daily
basis should be traceable back to an
annual or quarterly plan.
—*Richard E. Griggs*

Open confession is good for the soul.
—*Scottish Proverb*

The ultimate lesson all of us have to
learn is unconditional love,
which includes not only others but
ourselves as well.
—*Elisabeth Kubler-Ross*

He who cannot forgive breaks the
bridge over which he himself must pass.
—*George Herbert*

Go placidly amid the noise and haste
and remember what peace
there may be in silence.
—*Max Ehrmann*

Knowing what to say is not always
necessary; just the presence of a caring
friend can make a world of difference.
—*Sheri Curry*

Let me give so much time to the
improvement of myself that I shall have
no time to criticize others.
—*Dean Creshaw*

Jesus accepts you the way you are,
but loves you too much to
leave you that way.
—*Lee Venden*

Sometimes the best helping hand
you can give is a good, firm push.
—*Joann Thomas*

What I do today is important because
I am exchanging a day of my life for it.
—*Hugh Mulligan*

No matter how far you have gone on a
wrong road, turn back.
—*Turkish Proverb*

Enjoy the little things, for one day
you may look back and realize they
were the big things.
—*Robert Brault*

When words leave off,
music begins.
—*Heinrich Heine*

God never said it would be easy . . .
He just said He would go with me.
—*J. G. Holland*

If you are headed in the wrong
direction, God allows U-turns.
—*Author Unknown*

How long after you are gone will
ripples remain as evidence that you
were cast into the pool of life?
—*Grant M. Bright*

Here is the test to find whether your
mission on earth is finished:
If you're alive, it isn't.
—*Richard Bach*

Let us endeavor to live that when we
come to die even the undertaker
will be sorry.
—*Mark Twain*

Anytime you suffer a setback or
disappointment, put your head down
and plow ahead.
—*Les Brown*

Restlessness and discontent are the
necessities of progress.
—*Thomas Edison*

If you are losing your leisure, look out;
you may be losing your soul.
—*Author Unknown*

He does not seem to me to be a free man who does not sometimes do nothing.
—*Cicero*

Start living now. Stop saving the good china for that special occasion. Stop withholding your love until that special person materializes. Every day you are alive is a special occasion. Every minute, every breath, is a gift from God.
—*Mary Manin Morrissey*

The man who has no inner life is
the slave of his surroundings.
—*Henri Frederic Amiel*

All my possessions for a
moment of time.
—*Elizabeth I (last words)*

My father didn't tell me how to live; he
lived, and let me watch him do it.
—*Clarence Budinton Kelland*

There are only two lasting bequests we
can hope to give our children. One of
them is roots; the other, wings.
—*Hodding Carter*

All this trying leads up to the vital
moment at which you turn to God and
say, "You must do this. I can't."
—*C. S. Lewis*

The improving of our way of life is
more important than the spreading of
it. If we make it satisfactory enough, it
will spread automatically.
—*Charles A. Lindbergh*

Somewhere on this planet, someone
has a solution to each of the world's
problems. It might be one of us. With
your help, we can build a more
hopeful world.
—*Marianne Larned*

In every community there is work
to be done. In every nation there are
wounds to heal. In very heart there
is the power to do it.
—*Marianne Williamson*

It seldom happens that a man changes
his life through his habitual reasoning.
No matter how fully he may sense the
new plans and aims revealed to him by
reason, he continues to plod along in
old paths until his life becomes frustrat-
ing and unbearable—he finally makes
the change only when his usual life can
no longer be tolerated.
—*Leo Tolstoy*

Everyone must row
with the oars he has.
—*English Proverb*

You only grow by coming to the
end of something and by
beginning
something else.
—*John Irwin*

To be happy, drop the words "if only"
and substitute the words "next time."
—*Smiley Blanton*

The illusion of being superior
engenders the need to prove it,
and so oppression is born.
—*Jean Vanier*

People will not attend to what we say,
they will look carefully at what we do;
and they will say to us,
"First obey your own words and then
you can exhort others."
—*John Chrysosteom, Fourth Century*

Right now
Somebody needs your support.
Somebody needs you to have faith in
them. Somebody wants to be forgiven.
Somebody needs to know that your love
is unconditional.
—*Author Unknown*

Only those who risk going too far can
possibly find out how far they can go.
—*T. S. Elliot*

For every difficulty that supposedly
stops a person from succeeding there
are thousands who have had it a lot
worse and have succeeded anyway.
So can you.
—*Brian Tracy*

Outstanding people have one thing in
common: an absolute sense of mission.
—*Zig Ziglar*

Perfectionism is the voice of
the oppressor.
—*Anne Lamott*

Before you begin a thing, remind yourself that difficulties and delays quite
impossible to foresee are ahead. If you
could see them clearly, naturally you
could do a great deal to get rid of them
but you can't. You can only see one
thing clearly and that is your goal. Form
a mental vision of that and cling to it
through thick and thin.
—*Kathleen Norris*

Usefulness is not impaired by
imperfection. You can drink
from a chipped cup.
—*Greta K. Nagel*

Don't try to find Truth by looking
within yourself;
you're the one who's confused.
—*Frank Peretti*

If joy were the only emotion God
intended us to feel, He could just zap us
and take us to heaven right now. . . .
The truth is that our trials are a furnace
forging us into gold.
—*Barbara Johnson*

In the heat of an argument,
don't betray confidences;
word is sure to get around,
and no one will trust you.
—*King Solomon, Proverbs 25:9*

It has been my observation that people
are just about as happy as they make up
their minds to be.
—*Abraham Lincoln*

There is nothing we can do to make
God love us more,
There is nothing we can do to make
God love us less.
—*Philip Yancey*

Great horrors do not occur overnight,
nor do they develop in a vacuum. They
begin with small compromises,
unnoticed by most people.
—*Cal Thomas*

Good and evil both increase at com-
pound interest. That is why the little
decisions you and I make every day are
of such infinite importance.
—*C. S. Lewis*

It is common sense to take a method
and try it; if it fails, admit it frankly and
try another. But above all,
try something.
—*Franklin D. Roosevelt*

You can't have everything.
Where would you put it?
—*Steven Wright*

Seek those who are intelligent and
virtuous and if possible those who are
a little above you, especially in
moral excellence.
—*Stonewall Jackson*

It takes humility to seek feedback.
It takes wisdom to understand it,
analyze it, and appropriately
act on it.
—*Stephen Covey*

He who is ashamed of asking is
ashamed of learning.
—*Danish Proverb*

If you fall to pieces in a crisis,
there wasn't much to you in the
first place.
—*Precepts of the Sages, Proverbs 24:10*

Every now and again take a good look
at something not made with hands,
a mountain, a star, the turn of a stream.
There will come to you wisdom and
patience and solace and, above all,
the assurance that you are not
alone in the world.
—*Sidney Lovett*

The road must be trod, but it will be very hard. And neither strength nor wisdom will carry us far upon it. This quest may be attempted by the weak with as much hope as the strong. Yet such is oft the course of deeds that move the wheels of the world: small hands do them because they must, while the eyes of the great are elsewhere.

—*J. R. R. Tolkien*

A man doesn't begin to attain wisdom until he recognizes that he is no longer indispensable.

—*Admiral Richard E. Byrd*

The greatest and noblest pleasure which we have in this world is to discover new truths, and the next is to shake off old prejudices.
—*Frederick II, the Great*

The winter of the soul, in its seeming barrenness, its times of seeming unproductivity, its times of silence and seeming stalemate, is perhaps its most important season. Without it, there is no recovery of freshness and vitality, no bursting forth in springtime splendor.
—*Dwight Judy*

You can clutch the past so tightly
to your chest that it leaves your
arms too full to embrace the
present.
—*Jan Glidewell*

The best and most beautiful
things in the world cannot be seen
or even touched. They must be felt
with the heart.
—*Helen Keller*

The vision that you glorify in your
mind, the ideal that you enthrone in
your heart—this you will build your life
by, and this you will become.
—*James Lane Allen*

Every day above ground is a good one.
—*Malachy McCourt*

Give to every other human being every
right that you claim for yourself.
—*Robert Ingersoll*

Obstacles are those frightful things you
see when you take your eyes off
your goal.
—*Henry Ford*

Forget past mistakes. Forget failures.
Forget everything except what you are
going to do now and do it.
—*William Durant*

Quit now, you'll never make it. If you dis-
regard this advice, you'll be halfway there.
—*David Zucker*

The test of a successful person is not an
ability to eliminate all problems before
they arise, but to meet and work out difficulties when they do arise. We must be
willing to make an intelligent compromise with perfection lest we wait forever
before taking action. It's still good advice
to cross bridges as we come to them.
—*David Joseph Schwartz*

Mixed motives twist life into tangles;
pure motives take you straight
down the road.
—*King Solomon, Proverbs 21:8*

If your first concern is to look after
yourself, you'll never find yourself. But if
you forget about yourself and look to
me, you'll find both yourself and me.
—*Jesus, Matthew 10:39*

Right now
Somebody admires your strength
Somebody values your advice.
Somebody treasures your spirit.
Somebody thinks the world of you.
—*Author Unknown*

Last, but by no means least,
courage—moral courage,
the courage of one's convictions, the
courage to see things through. The
world is in a constant
conspiracy against the brave. It's the
age-old struggle—the roar of the
crowd on one side and the voice of
your conscience on
the other.
—*Douglas MacArthur*

Criticism is no doubt good for the
soul, but we must beware that it
does not upset our confidence
in ourselves.
—*Herbert Hoover*

Maturity is coming to terms with that
other part of yourself.
—*Ruth Tiffany Barnhouse*

Time is God's gift to me.
—*Kristen Johnson Ingram*

Fear of criticism is the kiss of death in
the courtship of achievement.
—*Author Unknown*

Sometimes all we have to do is get out
of the way.
—*Deborah Smith Douglas*

Wisdom calls us to a fierce
attention to reality.
—*Douglas Burton-Christie*

Life is this simple: we are living in a
world that is absolutely transparent and
God is shining through it all the time.
The only thing is that we don't see it.
—*Thomas Merton*

We bear the responsibility of
awakening others.
—*W. Paul Jones*

Hold nothing back.
—*Gerrit Scott Dawson*

Learn to embrace mystery.
—*Parker J. Palmer*

Letting go is not optional in this life, any more than exhaling is optional to breathing. What we call life is in fact a process of living and dying, attaching and detaching, going on at every moment.
—*Elaine M. Prevallet*

How much more grievous are the consequences of anger than the causes of it.
—*Marcus Aurelius Antoninus*

God is in the midst of the grief.
—*Gerrit Scott Dawson*

The way you live your life is your spiritual practice.
—*Robert C. Morris*

But be careful of distractions and the desire to do too many things at once. Above all things, be faithful to the present moment, doing one thing at a time, and you will receive all the grace you need.
—*François Fénelon*

Make time for your teen. Find an
activity you enjoy doing together and
pursue it. If your invitations are
declined, keep asking.
—*Sister Mary Rose McGready*

If you cannot do great things,
do small things in a great way.
—*Napoleon Hill*

Discipline your children while you still
have the chance; indulging them
destroys them.
—*King Solomon, Proverbs 19:18*

Tell the audience what you're going to
say, say it; then tell them what you've said.
—*Dale Carnegie*

The boundaries of a person's reality
often do not change until that person
forsakes what he or she feels confident
in and then goes blindly with faith.
—*Robert Kiyosaki*

People are where they are because that
is exactly where they really want to be—
whether they will admit that or not.
—*Earl Nightingale*

If you bungle raising your children, I
don't think whatever else you do well
matters very much.
—*Jacqueline Kennedy Onassis*

It takes courage to grow up and
become who you really are.
—*E. E. Cummings*

When you blame others, you give up
your power to change.
—*Robert Anthony*

Give sorrow words; the grief that does
not speak whispers the o'er-fraught
heart and bids it break.
—*William Shakespeare*

There will come a time when you
believe everything is finished. That will
be the beginning.
—*Louis L'Amour*

Hope begins in the dark, the stubborn hope that if you just show up and try to do the right thing, the dawn will come. You wait, and watch, and work, you don't give up.
—*Anne Lamott*

No really great man ever thought himself so.
—*William Hazlitt*

Among those whom I like or admire,
I can find no common denominator,
but among those who I love, I can:
all of them make me laugh.
—*W. H. Auden*

Don't judge each day by the harvest
you reap, but by the seeds you plant.
—*Robert Louis Stevenson*

Nothing makes us so lonely as
our secrets.
—*Paul Tournier*

Always there remain portions of our
heart into which no one is able to enter,
invite them as you may.
—*Mary Dixon Thayer*

Love is what is left over in a relationship after all the selfishness has been
removed.
—*Cullen Hightower*

Remember that everyone you meet is
afraid of something, loves something
and has lost something.
—*H. Jackson Brown Jr.*

If you don't express your own original
ideas, if you do not listen to your own
being, you will have betrayed yourself.
—*Rollo May*

Sometimes to remain silent is a lie.
—*Miguel de Unamuno*

When our views on the world and
your intellect are being challenged and
you begin to feel uncomfortable because
of a contradiction you've detected that
is threatening your current model of the
world or some aspect of it, pay attention. You are about to learn something.
—*William Drury*

Better to light a candle than
to curse the darkness.
—*Chinese Proverb*

The recipe for perpetual
ignorance is a very simple and
effective one: be satisfied with your
opinion and content with
your knowledge.
—*Elbert Hubbard*

You never find yourself until
you face the truth.
—*Pearl Bailey*

Right is right, even if everyone is against it, and wrong is wrong, even if everyone is for it.
—*William Penn*

To be nobody-but-yourself—in a world which is doing its best night and day, to make you everybody else—means to fight the hardest battle which any human being can fight, and never stop fighting.
—*E. E. Cummings*

Lie # 4: I can't be happy unless things go my way.
—*Chris Thurman*

Some people are making such
thorough preparation for rainy days that
they aren't enjoying today's sunshine.
—*William Feather*

Bravery is not what you feel but what
you make up your mind to do.
—*Patsy Clairmont*

The true secret of giving advice is,
after you have honestly given it, to be
perfectly indifferent whether it is taken
or not, and never persist in trying
to set people right.
—*Hannah Whitall Smith*

If I could live my life again, I'd spend more time fully involved in the present moment, less time remembering and anticipating. I'd be more aware of my core values and life mission, and less concerned with the reasons why I might not measure up.

—*Author Unknown*

When you've done what needs to be done, go ahead and do a little more. When you've gotten some momentum going, make good use of it.

—*Ralph Marston*

Love and truth form a good
leader;
sound leadership is founded on
loving integrity.
—*King Solomon, Proverbs 20:28*

Beneath the responsibilities and
demands of daily living we feel a
summoning to something more.
The pleasures, privileges, and
pursuits of this world have not
satisfied it. Religion and religious
activity is not quenching it. This
summoning is the invitation of
Jesus to know him as our lives.
—*Pat DePalma*

Everything occurring in a family,
regardless of how carefully it may be
hidden, impacts the children.
Everything.
—*Robert Hemfelt*

We become just by performing just
actions, temperate by performing temperate actions, brave by performing
brave actions.
—*Aristotle*

Think of all the beauty still left around
you and be happy.
—*Anne Frank*

The first step in releasing the past is to become aware of the problems that still exist. Identify what is from your past that still bothers you, affects you, influences you, or hinders you.
—*H. Norman Wright*

But think about who your anger is hurting most: you.
—*Anne F. Grizzle*

You will know that forgiveness has begun when you recall those who hurt you and feel the power to wish them well.
—*Lewis B. Smedes*

Not everything that is faced can be
changed, but nothing can be changed
until it is faced.
—*James Baldwin*

How unhappy is he who cannot
forgive himself.
—*Publilius Syrus*

An impulsive vow is a trap;
later you'll wish you could get out of it.
—*King Solomon, Proverbs 20:25*

Change is the only constant.
Hanging on is the only sin.
—*Denise McCluggage*

Never put your trust in slogans.
—*Slogan*

Joy is not the absence of suffering
but the presence of God.
—*Elisabeth Elliot*

Beware of paying attention or going
back to what you once were,
when God wants you to be something
that you have never been.
—*Oswald Chambers*

Patient persistence pierces through
indifference;
gentle speech breaks down rigid
defenses.
—*King Solomon, Proverbs 25:15*

Don't fall victim to the "ready-aim-
aim-aim-aim syndrome." You must be
willing to fire.
—*T. Boone Pickens*

Don't be afraid to take a big step if
one is indicated. You can't cross a
chasm in two small jumps.
—*David Loyd George*

No great man ever complains of want
of opportunity.
—*Ralph Waldo Emerson*

No man knows what he can do
till he tries.
—*Publilius Syrus*

Call your mom.
—*Author Unknown*

The only difference between a rut and
a grave is their dimensions.
—*Ellen Glasgow*

When you soar like an eagle, you
attract the hunters.
—*Milton S. Gould*

A single lie destroys a whole reputation
of integrity.
—*Baltasar Gracian*

Don't fix the blame, fix the problem.
—*Keith S. Pennington*

You can't be big and little at the same time. If you're going to be magnanimous, you can't also be stingy.
—*M. N. Young Sr.*

In actual life every great enterprise begins with and takes its first forward step in faith.
—*Frederich von Schlegel*

A man is not old until regrets
take the place of dreams.
—*John Barrymore*

At any given moment, you can choose
a different path; the choice is yours.
—*Author Unknown*

It is a wholesome and necessary thing
for us to turn again to the earth and in
the contemplation of her beauties to
know of wonder and humility.
—*Rachel Carson*

Since Jesus went through everything
you're going through and more,
learn to think like him.
—*Saint Peter, 1 Peter 4:1*

We have all known the long loneliness
and we have learned that the only solution is love and that love comes with
community.
—*Dorothy Day*

How wonderful it is that nobody need
wait a single moment before starting
to improve the world.
—*Anne Frank*

Persons are to be loved,
things are to be used.
—*Reuel Howe*

There are no problems we cannot solve together, and very few we can solve by ourselves.
—*Lyndon B. Johnson*

We tend to forget that happiness does not come as a result of getting something we don't have, but rather of recognizing and appreciating what we do have.
—*Frederick Koenig*

Whenever we decide to change, we meet resistance. We are always challenged to see if we are serious.
—*Andrew Matthews*

Change is inevitable,
growth is intentional.
—*Glenda Cloud*

There is no royal road to anything. One thing at a time, all
things in succession. That which
grows slowly endures.
—*Josiah G. Holland*

It takes wisdom and discernment to
minister to people in need. We must
look beyond the apparent and seek to
meet the needs of the whole person.
—*Richard C. Chewning*

Be brave enough to accept
the help of others.
—*Peter McWilliams*

He who waits to do a great deal of
good at once, will never do anything.
—*Samuel Johnson*

Is anyone crying for help? God is
listening, ready to rescue you. If your
heart is broken, you'll find God right
there; if you're kicked in the gut,
he'll help you catch your breath.
—*King David, Psalms 34:17*

The holiest of all holidays are those
kept by ourselves in silence and apart;
the secret anniversaries of the heart.
—*Henry Wadsworth Longfellow*

Let my heart be broken with the things
that break the heart of God.
—*Bob Pierce*

Revenge never healed a wound.
—*Guarino Guarini*

Vulnerability means that we let go of
protective mechanisms that close us to
the possibility of being deeply influ-
enced by others.
—*Katherine Zappone*

The ability to find joy in the sorrow
and hope at the edge of despair is
woman's witness to courage and
her gift of new life to all.
—*Miriam Therese Winter*

Every word and deed of a parent
is a fiber woven into the character
of a child, which ultimately deter-
mines how that child fits into the
fabric of society.
—*David Wilkerson*

Don't walk in front of me;
I may not follow.
Don't walk behind me;
I may not lead.
Just walk beside me
and be my friend.
—*Author Unknown*

Perhaps we have done everything in the world to find health and radiance, happiness and peace, except to listen to, and heed the soul, crying always that same plaintive cry, the cry of the stream for the ocean, the cry of the prisoner for freedom, the cry of the wanderer for home, the cry of the starving for food, the cry of the soul for God.
—*Leslie Weatherhead*

Malice backfires; spite boomerangs.
—*King Solomon, Proverbs 26:27*

Great beginnings are not as important as the way one finishes.
—*James Dobson*

You can never establish a personal relationship without opening up your own heart.
—*Paul Tournier*

Tell me how much you know of the sufferings of your fellow man and I will tell you how much you have loved them.
—*Helmut Thielicke*

We must be confident that there
is still more "life" to be "lived" and yet
more heights to be scaled. The tragedy
of middle age is that, so often, men and
women cease to press "towards the
goal of their high calling". They cease
learning, cease growing, they give
up and resign from life.
—*Evelyn Sturge*

Love not only prefers the good of
another to my own, but it does not
even compare the two.
—*Thomas Merton*

Death is what takes place within
us when we look upon others not
as a gift, blessing or stimulus but as
threat, danger, competition. It is
not the final departure we think of
when we speak of death; it is that
purposeless, empty existence
devoid of genuine human relationships and filled with anxiety,
silence and loneliness.

—*Dorothee Soelle*

To pray about any day's work does not mean to ask for success in it. It means, first to realize my own inability to do even a familiar job, as it truly should be done, unless I am in touch with eternity, unless I do it "unto God," unless I have the Father with me.
—*Mary F. Smith*

Passion, for all its dangers, needs uncaging if we are to move towards completeness as human beings.
—*Philip Sheldrake*

God does not love us because we are valuable. We are valuable because God loves us.
—*Fulton John Sheen*

Every day the choice between good
and evil is presented to us in
simple ways.
—*W. E. Sangster*

Often nothing requires more courage
than admission of fault.
—*Joan Puls*

To love is to be willing to put the
beloved in the first place and oneself in
the second place.
—*Norman Pittenger*

As we separate everyday life from religion, we are breaking up the unity and
wholeness of life.
—*Akin J. Omoyajowo*

No human being can understand us
fully, no human being can give us
unconditional love, no human being can
offer constant affection, no human
being can enter into the core of our
being and heal our deepest brokenness.
—*Henri Nouwen*

Life is filled with meaning as soon as
Jesus Christ enters it.
—*Stephen Neil*

I don't think that television has conquered me. But I do think that man has
invented it to flee from reality.
—*Malcolm Muggeridge*

Wear the old coat and buy the
new book.
—*Austin Phelps*

I have an idea that laughter is able
to mediate between the infinite
magnitude of our tasks and the
limitation of our strength.
—*Jürgen Moltmann*

When you have to make a vital
decision about behaviour, you cannot
sit on the fence. To decide to do nothing
is still a decision, and it means that you
remain on the station platform or the
air strip when the train or plane has left.
—*Kathleen Lonsdale*

Whatever you have, spend less.
—*Samuel Johnson*

If you don't get close to people
you can't love them.
—*Bill Kirkpatrick*

The habit of thinking ill of everything
and everyone is tiresome to ourselves
and to all around us.
—*Pope John XXIII*

We can do nothing if we hate
ourselves, or feel that all our actions
are doomed to failure because of
our own worthlessness.
—*Martin Israel*

There are no more tragic figures in life
and in literature than the cold and lonely
figures who are so afraid of the fires in
their own hearts that they would put
them out rather than run the danger
of being burned by them.
—*Richard Holloway*

Each of us will have our own different
ways of expressing love and care for the
family. But unless that is a high priority,
we may find that we may gain the whole
world and lose our own children.
—*Michael Green*

The virtue of moderation can be
understood as a balancing of patience
and impatience, action and reflection,
haste and caution, compromise
and polarization.
—*Father Tissa Balasuriya*

Near to losing heart? Are you overborne with labour? Or worn out with worry? Or consumed with hopeless longings? Don't try to keep the whole thing pent up within your own heart.
—*John Baillie*

We have forgotten that to be radical means simply to go to the root of things.
—*Rubem Alves*

Why do we say no? In order to say yes
to what really matters.
—*Miriam Adeney*

Nothing is certain: everything is safe.
—*Charles Williams*

We spent most of our lives
conjugating three verbs: to want,
to have and to do. But none of these
verbs has any ultimate significance until
it is transcended by and included in the
fundamental verb—to be.
—*Evelyn Underhill*

When you love someone,
you love him as he is.
—*Charles Peguy*

The real measure of our wealth is how much we'd be worth if we lost all our money.
—*John Hewitt Jowett*

Be silent about great things, let them grow inside you.
—*Friedrich von Hugel*

I won't waste more time hating myself.
—*Temple Gairdner*

An open word spoken directly to another person deepens friendship and is not resented.
—*Eberhard Arnold*

It is a splendid habit to laugh
inwardly at yourself.
—*Henri de Tourville*

There never has been, and cannot be,
a good life without self-control.
—*Leo Tolstoy*

What is morally wrong can never be
politically right.
—*Anthony Ashley Cooper, Earl of Shaftesbury*

Have great care of your children.
We live in a time when much freedom is given to the expression of
thought, but little care is taken that
thoughts should be founded on the
truth. Teach them to love truth.
—*Macarius of Optino*

You have been used to take
notice of the wayings of dying
men. This is mine: that a life spent
in the service of God, and com-
munion with him, is the most
comfortable and pleasant life that
anyone can live in the world.
—*Matthew Henry*

There are two freedoms—the false,
where a man is free to do what he likes;
the true, where a man is free to do what
he ought.
—*Charles Kingsley*

When angry, count ten before you speak;
if very angry, count to one hundred.
—*Thomas Jefferson*

The essence of a perfect friendship is
that each friend reveals himself utterly
to the other, flings aside his reserves,
and shows himself for who he truly is.
—*Robert Hugh Benson*

Refrain from reprimanding your children while you are in this condition of rage. It will be better for you, and more impressive for them if you talk things over calmly, a little later.
—*Macarius of Optino*

It is a rough road that leads to the heights of greatness.
—*Seneca*

Success: The conscientious stewarding of the next generation.
—*Tim Kimmel*

Whoever wants to embrace life and
see the day fill up with good, here's
what you do: say nothing evil or hurtful;
snub evil and cultivate good; run after
peace for all you're worth.
—*Saint Peter, 1 Peter 3:10–11*

Time is precious. You can't own it, but
you can use it. You can't keep it, but you
can spend it. Once you've lost it, you
can never have it back.
—*Harvey Mackay*

No medicine is more valuable, none more efficacious, none better suited to the cure of all our temporal ills than a friend to whom we may turn for consolation in time of trouble—and with whom we may share our happiness in time of joy.
——*Saint Aelred of Rievaulx,*
Twelfth Century

A desk is a dangerous place from which to view the world.
—*John LeCarre*

This is as true in everyday life as it is in battle: we are given one life and the decision is ours whether to wait for circumstances to make up our mind, or whether to act and, in acting, to live.
—*Omar Bradley*

99 percent of the game is half mental.
—*Yogi Berra*

Sometimes you gotta create what you want to be a part of.
—*Geri Weitzman*

Everybody wants to save the earth; nobody wants to help Mom do the dishes.
—*P. J. O'Rourke*

A pessimist sees the difficulty in every opportunity; an optimist sees the opportunity in every difficulty.
—*Winston Churchill*

F ocus 90 percent of your time on solutions and only 10 percent of your time on problems.
—*Anthony J. D'Angelo*

T o gain that which is worth having, it may be necessary to lose everything else.
—*Bernadette Devlin*

Don't wear yourself out trying
to get rich; restrain yourself! Riches
disappear in the blink of an eye;
wealth sprouts wings and flies off
into the wild blue yonder.
—*Precepts of the Sages, Proverbs 23:4–5*

He is a fool who leaves things close at
hand to follow what is out of reach.
—*Plutarch*

I kept on digging the hole deeper and
deeper looking for the treasure chest
until I finally lifted my head, looked up
and realized that I had dug
my own grave.
—*Author Unknown*

We who lived in concentration camps can remember the men who walked throughout the huts comforting others, giving away their last piece of bread. They may have been few in number, but they offer sufficient proof that everything can be taken away from a man but one thing: the last of the human freedoms—to choose one's attitude in any given set of circumstances, to choose one's own way.

—*Viktor Frankl*

Oh, my friend, it's not what they take
away from you that counts. It's what
you do with what you have left.
—*Hubert Humphrey*

Do, or do not. There is no try.
—*George Lucas*

Why not go out on a limb? That's
where the fruit is.
—*Will Rogers*

Try a thing you haven't done three
times. Once, to get over the fear of
doing it. Twice, to learn how to do it.
And a third time, to figure out
whether you like it or not.
—*Virgil Thomson*

Friendship is born at that moment
when one person says to another,
"What! You too? I thought I
was the only one."
—*C. S. Lewis*

There's an opportune time to do
things, a right time for everything on
the earth . . . a right time to hold on
and a right time to let go.
—*King Solomon, Ecclesiastes 3:1, 6*

Twenty years from now you will be
more disappointed by the things you
didn't do than by the ones you did do. So
throw off the bowlines. Sail away from
the safe harbor. Catch the trade winds in
your sails. Explore. Dream. Discover.
—*Mark Twain*

If you want to make enemies, try to
change something.
—*Woodrow Wilson*

Official Project Stages:
(1) Uncritical Acceptance.
(2) Wild Enthusiasm
(3) Dejected Disillusionment.
(4) Total Confusion.
(5) Search for the Guilty.
(6) Punishment of the Innocent.
(7) Promotion of the
Non-participants.
—*Author Unknown*

A single conversation across the
table with a wise man is worth a
month's study of books.
—*Chinese Proverb*

Don't hang out with angry people,
don't keep company with hotheads.
Bad temper is contagious—
don't get infected.
—*Precepts of the Sages, Proverbs 22:24–25*

You cannot discover new oceans
unless you have the courage to
lose sight of the shore.
—*Author Unknown*

Don't let fear stop you.
—*William F. Light*

If you knew the generosity of God and
who I am, you would be asking me for a
drink, and I would give you fresh,
living water.
—*Jesus, John 4:10*

To accomplish great things, you must
not only act but also dream, not only
dream but also believe.
—*Anatole France*

The chief danger in life is that you
may take too many precautions.
—*Alfred Adler*

Life is not lost by dying; life is lost
minute by minute, day by dragging day,
in all the thousand small uncaring ways.
—*Stephen Vincent Benét*

Be polite to all, but intimate with few.
—*Thomas Jefferson*

The reverse side also has a reverse side.
—*Japanese Proverb*

Use your discernment and choose
the course which takes you farthest
away from the deadening activities
of the stifling world, and brings
you close to God.
—*Babai the Great, Syriac Monk,
Sixth Century*

Speak the truth, but
leave immediately after.
—*Slovenian Proverb*

Is is opposition that makes us
productive.
—*Johann Wolfgang von Goethe*

How many things I can do without!
—*Socrates*

Always and never are two words you
should always remember never to use.
—*Wendell Johnson*

There is no substitute for
paying attention.
—*Diane Sawyer*

Never take a cross country trip with a
kid who has just learned to whistle.
—*Jean Deuel*

To want in one's head to do a thing
for its own sake, to enjoy doing it,
to concentrate all of one's energies
upon it—that is not only the surest
guarantee of its success. It is also
being true to oneself.
—*Amelia Earhart*

Don't ask yourself what the world
needs, ask yourself what makes you
come alive, and then go and do that.
Because what the world needs is
people who have come alive.
—*Harold Whitman*

If you want help, help others. If you want trust, trust others. If you want love, give it away. If you want friends, be one. If you want a great team, be a great teammate. That's how it works.
—*Dan Zadra*

Very few people are ambitious in the sense of having a specific image of what they want to achieve. Most people's sights are only toward the next run, the next increment of money.
—*Judith M. Bardwick*

Keep away from people who try
to belittle your ambitions. Small
people always do that, but the
really great make you feel that you,
too, can become great.
—*Mark Twain*

✳

Though no one can go back and
make a brand new start, anyone
can start from now and make a
brand new ending.
—*Carl Bard*

An error is not a mistake until you
refuse to correct it.
—*Author Unknown*

If you limit your choices only to what
seems possible or reasonable, you dis-
connect yourself from what you truly
want, and all that is left is a
compromise.
—*Robert Fritz*

The man who has begun to live more
seriously within begins to live more
simply without.
—*Phillips Brooks*

Act as if what you do makes a
difference. It does.
—*William James*

Cautious, careful people,
always casting about to preserve
their reputations . . . can never
effect a reform.
—*Susan B. Anthony*

We work to feed our appetites,
meanwhile our souls go hungry.
—*King Solomon, Ecclesiastes 6:7*

People will accept your ideas much
more readily if you tell them that
Benjamin Franklin said it first.
—*Author Unknown*

Very often a change of self is needed
more than a change of scene.
—*Arthur Christopher Benson*

Let everyone be important in your
eyes, and do not despise those whose
knowledge is less than yours.
—*John of Apamea*

Don't believe all you hear, spend all
you have, or sleep all you want.
—*Author Unknown*

One of the incredible blind spots
we humans seem to have is that we
can walk down the same path each
day and expect to come out at a
different location. We don't stop to
think that if we want different
results, we have to do something
different than we have been
to achieve it.
—*Dennis Gaskill*

The difficulty lies not in the new
ideas but in escaping from the
old ones.
—*John Maynard Keynes*

Don't ask the barber whether you
need a haircut.
—*Daniel S. Greenberg*

The last time you failed, did you stop
trying because you failed—or did you
fail because you stopped trying?
—*Author Unknown*

However beautiful the strategy, you
should occasionally look at the results.
—*Winston Churchill*

You might have to fight a battle more
than once to win it.
—*Margaret Thatcher*

That's the risk you take if you change,
that people you've been involved with
won't like the new you. But other people
who do will come along.
—*Lisa Alther*

Every great mistake has a halfway
moment, a split second when it can be
recalled and perhaps remedied.
—*Pearl S. Buck*

Life is change. Growth is optional.
Choose wisely.
—*Karen Kaiser Clark*

If you don't like the way the world is,
you change it. You have an obligation to
change it. You just do it one step
at a time.
—*Marian Wright Edelman*

Power is the ability not to have to
please.
—*Elizabeth Janeway*

All my life I've wanted to be somebody.
But I see now I should have been
more specific.
—*Jane Wagner*

There is nothing so fatal to character
than half-finished tasks.
—*David Loyd George*

Lose nothing for want of asking.
—*Ancient Proverb*

Most of our assumptions have
outlived their usefulness.
—*Marshall McLuhan*

Look at everything as though
you were seeing it either for the first
or last time. Then your time on earth
will be filled with glory.
—*Betty Smith*

Acceptance of what has happened
is the first step to overcoming the
consequences of misfortune.
—*William James*

Do not cut down the tree
that gives you shade.
—*Persian Proverb*

Reflect on your present blessings—
of which every man has many—
not on your past misfortunes,
of which all men have some.
—*Charles Dickens*

Disconnecting from change does not
recapture the past. It loses the future.
—*Kathleen Norris*

Talk less and say more.
—*Vermont Proverb*

If it ain't broke, don't fix it.
—*Bert Lance*

If it ain't broke, break it.
—*Robert J. Kriegel and Louis Palter*

Anyone who is not burning will not be able to set anyone else on fire first.
—*Peter of Rheims, French Dominican Friar, Thirteenth Century*

Don't worry over what other people are thinking about you. They're too busy worrying about what you are thinking about them.
—*Author Unknown*

How easy it is to fall into the illusion of a beautiful world when we have lost trust in our capacity to make our broken world a place that can become more beautiful.
—*Jean Vanier*

Don't put the cart before
the horse.
—*Latin Proverb*

Before you clean up the world,
think about your garage.
—*Author Unknown*

Don't jump to conclusions.
—*Ancient Proverb*

One day at a time.
—*Slogan of Alcoholics Anonymous*

If you wait, all that happens is that
you get older.
—*Larry McMurtry*

When in doubt, do without.
—*Vermont Proverb*

Don't push your way to the front; don't sweet-talk your way to the top. Put yourself aside, and help others get ahead. Don't be obsessed with getting your own advantage. Forget yourselves long enough to lend a helping hand.
—*St. Paul, Philippians 2:3–4*

Sometimes the most urgent and vital thing you can do is take a complete rest.
—*Ashleigh Brilliant*

Never forget the three powerful resources you always have available to you: love, prayer, and forgiveness.
—*H. Jackson Brown Jr.*

Every man should have a fair-sized
cemetery in which to bury the
faults of his friends.
—*Henry Ward Beecher*

Age is only a number.
—*Lexi Starling*

The most life-destroying word of all
is the word tomorrow.
—*Robert Kiyosaki*

Self-pity in its early stages is as
snug as a feather mattress.
Only when it hardens does it
become uncomfortable.
—*Maya Angelou*

Don't be rushed into making an
important decision. People will
understand if you say, "I'd like a
little more time to think it over.
Can I get back to you tomorrow?"
—*H. Jackson Brown Jr.*

Nothing valuable can be lost
by taking time.
—*Abraham Lincoln*

Ideas are like children—if you don't
send them out into the world,
they die with you.
—*Jacob L. Moreno*

Lie # 5: It's somebody else's fault.
—*Chris Thurman*

If you tell the truth you don't have
to remember anything.
—*Mark Twain*

Once a year, go someplace you've
never been before.
—*Author Unknown*

When one is a stranger to oneself, then
one is estranged from others too.
—*Anne Morrow Lindbergh*

To be conscious that you are ignorant
is a great step to knowledge.
—*Benjamin Disraeli*

It's never too late to mend.
—*Ancient Proverb*

No man can succeed in a line of
endeavor which he does not like.
—*Napoleon Hill*

Do the hard jobs first. The easy jobs
will take care of themselves.
—*Dale Carnegie*

To do nothing is sometimes a
good remedy.
—*Hippocrates*

In the game of life, heredity deals the
hand, society makes the rules, but you
can still play your own cards.
—*Peter's Almanac*

Yesterday is a cancelled check,
tomorrow is a promissory note,
today is ready cash—use it.
—*Kay Lyons*

Many a false step is taken
by standing still.
—*Arnold Glasow*

Love's finest speech
is without words.
—*Hadewijch of Brabant*

He is wise who knows what is enough.
—*Japanese Proverb*

The best combination of parents
consists of a father who is gentle
beneath his firmness, and a mother
who is firm beneath her gentleness.
—*Sydney J. Harris*

Of all the excuses this is most morbid:
"I did the thing because the others did."
—*Arthur Guiterman*

One way to get high blood pressure is
to go mountain climbing over molehills.
—*Earl Wilson*

Music washes away from the soul the
dust of every-day life.
—*Berthold Auerbach*

You grow up the day you have your
first real laugh at yourself.
—*Ethel Barrymore*

Don't be afraid to say, "I don't know."
Don't be afraid to say, "I made a
mistake." Don't be afraid to say,
"I need help."
Don't be afraid to say, "I'm sorry."
—*H. Jackson Brown Jr.*

Pretending to be perfect when you
know you're not, can be exhausting.
—*Nancy Drew*

Fun is the safety-valve that lets the
steam-pressure off from the boiler, and
keeps things from busting.
—*Josh Billings*

I would suggest two things. First of all,
never try to justify yourself before God.
And second, do not condemn yourself.
Instead, why not quietly lay your
imperfections before God?
—*Françoise Fénelon*

If you don't get what you want,
it is a sign either that you did not
seriously want it, or that you tried
to bargain over the price.
—*Rudyard Kipling*

Gossips break up friendships.
—*King Solomon, Proverbs 16:28*

There is always an easy solution to
every human problem—simple,
plausible, and wrong.
—*H. L. Mencken*

Grain by grain, a loaf of bread;
stone by stone, a castle.
—*Yugoslavian Proverb*

If opportunity has shut one door,
resolve can open thrice a
hundred more.
—*Arthur Guiterman*

A man who trims himself to suit
everybody will soon whittle himself
to nothing.
—*Charles Schwab*

The ability to say no is more valuable
to a man than the ability to read Latin.
—*William C. Hunter*

Asking dumb questions is easier than
correcting dumb mistakes.
—*Author Unknown*

I never ask the wounded person how he
feels; I myself become the
wounded person.
—*Walt Whitman*

We have left undone those things
which we ought to have done;
and we have done those things
which we ought not to have done.
—*Book of Common Prayer*

Never put off till tomorrow
what you can put off for good.
—*Author Unknown*

Hear the other side.
—*Latin Proverb*

It might be a good idea to ask ourselves
how we develop our capacity to choose
for joy. Maybe we could spend a
moment at the end of each day and
decide to remember that day—whatever
may have happened—as a day to be
grateful for.
—*Henri Nouwen*

The library is the temple of learning,
and learning has liberated more people
than all the wars in history.
—*Carl Rowan*

When I was a young man
I vowed never to marry until I
found the ideal woman. Well, I
found her but, alas, she was waiting for the ideal man.
—*Robert Schuman*

All lay a load on the
willing horse.
—*George Heywood*

Spend at least an hour a week in a natural setting, away from crowds of people, traffic, and buildings. There is nothing more basic, more simple, than the natural world.
—*Linda Breen Pierce*

The beginning of wisdom is calling things by their right names.
—*Chinese Proverb*

Look for a reason to need people, and they will need you in return.
—*M. Norvel Young*

The dissenter is every human being at
those moments of his life when he
resigns momentarily from the herd
and thinks for himself.
—*Archibald MacLeish*

Kindle not a fire that you
cannot extinguish.
—*African Proverb*

The door to success is always marked
Push.
—*Author Unknown*

No one ever excused his way
to success.
—*David del Dotto*

Said first and thought after
Brings many to disaster.
—*H. W. Thompson*

What wound did ever heal
but by degrees?
—*William Shakespeare*

Do not pray for easy lives. Pray to be
stronger men. Do not pray for tasks
equal to your powers. Pray for power
equal to your tasks.
—*Phillips Brooks*

When someone else writes your script,
you're not living. You're just
playing a part.
—*Donald G. Smith*

The truth hurts . . . Not the
searching after, the running from.
—*John Eyberg*

The wheel that squeaks the
loudest is the one that gets the
grease . . . and the wheel that
makes too much of a nuisance
of itself gets replaced.
—*Author Unknown*

A happy marriage is the world's
best bargain.
—*O. A. Battista*

There is no stigma attached to
recognizing a bad decision in time
to install a better one.
—*Laurence Peter*

Don't let the fear of the time it will take
to accomplish something stand in the
way of your doing it. The time will pass
anyway; we might just as well put that
passing time to the best possible use.
—*Earl Nightingale*

Any man who thinks he's smarter than
his wife is married to a smart woman.
—*Author Unknown*

Don't let any material thing come into
your home unless you absolutely love it
and want to keep it until it is
beyond repair.
—*Linda Breen Pierce*

Do things for others and you'll find
your self-consciousness evaporating
like morning dew on a Missouri
cornfield in July.
—*Dale Carnegie*

Spoken words fly away;
written words remain.
—*Latin Proverb*

Never be afraid to try something new.
Remember, amateurs built the ark.
Professionals built the *Titanic*.
—*Author Unknown*

Teachers open the door,
but you must enter by yourself.
—*Chinese Proverb*

Rules of the road: Too much concern
for safety is dangerous.
—*Judy Cannato*

307

After you have formed an acquaintance with an individual, never allow it to draw to a close without a cause.

—*Stonewall Jackson*

You can't take it with you.

—*Ancient Proverb*

We forfeit three-fourths of ourselves
to be like other people.
—*Arthur Schopenhauer*

The Lord sends no one away empty
except those who are full of themselves.
—*Dwight L. Moody*

There is no pillow so soft as a
clear conscience.
—*French Proverb*

There's no limit to what can be
accomplished if it doesn't matter
who gets the credit.
—*Author Unknown*

When fate hands you a lemon,
make lemonade.
—*Dale Carnegie*

It is a characteristic of wisdom not to
do desperate things.
—*Henry David Thoreau*

One ought never to turn one's back on
a threatened danger and try to run
away from it. If you do that, you double
the danger. But if you meet it promptly
and without flinching, you will reduce
the danger by half. Never run away
from anything. Never!
—*Winston Churchill*

He is your friend who pushes you
nearer to God.
—*Abraham Kuyper*

Never look back unless you are
planning to go that way.
—*Author Unknown*

Everyone is a house with four rooms . . .
physical . . . mental . . . emotional . . .
spiritual . . . and unless we go into each
room each day, even if only to keep it
aired, we are not a complete person.
—*Rumer Godden*

The world's best reformers are those
who begin on themselves.
—*George Bernard Shaw*

So if you find life difficult because
you're doing what God said, take
it in stride. Trust him. He knows
what he's doing.
—*St. Peter, 1 Peter 4:19*

We can learn even from
our enemies.
—*Ovid*

Remember that the best relationship is one where your love for each other is greater than your need for each other.
—*Author Unknown*

Once you begin to explain or excuse all events on racial grounds, you begin to indulge in the perilous mythology of race.
—*James Earl Jones*

You lose a lot of time, hating people.
—*Marian Anderson*

For finally, we are as we love. It is love that measures our stature.
—*William Sloane Coffin*

Yesterday is gone.
Tomorrow has not yet come.
We have only today.
Let us begin.
—*Mother Teresa*

If you're never scared or
embarrassed or hurt, it means you
never take any chances.
—*Julia Sorel*

You cannot achieve the impossible
without attempting the absurd.
—*Author Unknown*

The fire which seems extinguished
often slumbers beneath the ashes.
—*Pierre Corneille*

The ordinary acts we practice every
day at home are of more importance to
the soul than their simplicity
might suggest.
—*Thomas Moore*

Many pious people would rather study
the Bible than practice what it teaches.
—*Author Unknown*

If you cultivate a healthy poverty
and simplicity, so that finding a penny
will literally make your day, then, since
the world is in fact planted in pennies,
you have with your poverty bought
a lifetime of days.
—*Annie Dillard*

Nothing great is created suddenly.
—*Epictetus*

Envy is the father and mother of
many hideous monsters.
—*John Bunyan*

In the long run men hit only
what they aim at.
—*Henry David Thoreau*

It's the soul's duty to be loyal to its own
desires. It must abandon itself to its
master passion.
—*Rebecca West*

In the rush and noise of life, as you
have intervals, step within yourselves
and be still. Wait upon God and feel his
good presence; this will carry you
through your day's business.
—*William Penn*

No matter how much pressure you feel
at work, if you could find ways to relax
for at least five minutes every hour,
you'd be more productive.
—*Joyce Brothers*

Nothing can be done at once hastily
and prudently.
—*Pliny*

No entertainment is so cheap as
reading, nor any pleasure more lasting.
—*Lady Mary Wortley Montagu*

I would advise you to read with a pen
in your hand, and enter in a little book
short hints of what you find that is
curious, or that might be useful;
for this will be the best method of
imprinting such particulars in your
memory, where they will be ready,
on some future occasion.
—*Benjamin Franklin*

A man is known
by the promises he keeps.
—*Ancient Proverb*

The tighter you squeeze,
the less you have.
—*Thomas Merton*

Instead of going to Paris to attend lectures, go to the public library, and you won't come out for twenty years, if you really wish to learn.
—*Leo Tolstoy*

If I could live my life again, I'd walk in the rain more without an umbrella and listen less to weather reports. I'd spend much more time outdoors in small towns and less time in tall buildings and big cities. I'd eat more of everything healthy and delicious, less of everything each meal, saving enough on the bill to feed a starving child.
—*Author Unknown*

The only fence against the world is a
thorough knowledge of it.
—*John Locke*

Until you have learned to be tolerant
with those who do not always agree
with you, until you have cultivated the
habit of saying some kind word of
those whom you do not admire,
until you have formed the habit of
looking for the good instead of the
bad there is in others, you will be
neither successful nor happy.
—*Napoleon Hill*

There are four steps to accomplishment: Plan purposefully. Prepare prayerfully. Proceed positively. Pursue persistently.
—*Author Unknown*

Out of the wreck I rise.
—*Robert Browning*

Live in the world you inhabit. Look upon things as they are. Take them as you find them. Make the best of them. Turn them to your advantage.
—*Robert E. Lee*

Take a good look at the opportunities
and abilities you have in the place in life
where God has put you.
—*John Bunyan*

It's difficult to inspire others to accomplish what you haven't been willing to try.
—*Author Unknown*

A sparkling house is a fine thing if
the children aren't robbed of their
luster in keeping it that way.
—*Marcelene Cox*

Rules of the road: It is permissible to
ask for directions.
—*Judy Cannato*

If I were asked to give what I
consider the single most useful bit
of advice for all humanity it would
be this: Expect trouble as an
inevitable part of life and when it
comes, hold your head high, look
it squarely in the eye and say,
"I will be bigger than you.
You cannot defeat me."
—*Ann Landers*

You can never get much of anything done unless you go ahead
and do it before you are ready.
—*Author Unknown*

No one knows what he can do
till he tries.
—*Pliny*

How much time he gains who does not
look to see what his neighbor says or
does or thinks, but only at what he does
himself, to make it just and holy.
—*Marcus Aurelius Antoninus*

Whatever is begun in anger
ends in shame.
—*George Eliot*

I do not believe in a fate that falls on
men however they act, but I do believe
in a fate that falls on them unless
they act.
—*G. K. Chesterton*

God whispers to us in our pleasures,
speaks in our conscience, but shouts
in our pain: it is His megaphone
to rouse a deaf world.
—*C. S. Lewis*

Never judge a man's actions
until you know his motives.
—*Author Unknown*

Listen, really listen. Because parents have so much to do and so little time, we often try to listen while cleaning, washing dishes, or fixing the car. Put your chores aside so your teen knows you're really paying attention.

—*Sister Mary Rose McGready*

All progress is due to those who were not satisfied to let well enough alone.

—*Author Unknown*

How far you go in life
depends on your being tender
with the young, compassionate
with the aged, sympathetic with
the striving, and tolerant of the
weak and strong. Because
someday in your life you will
have been all of these.
—*George Washington Carver*

You must take action now that
will move you towards your goals.
Develop a sense of urgency
in your life.
—*H. Jackson Brown Jr.*

The life which is unexamined
is not worth living.
—*Plato*

People are won to your religious
beliefs less by description than by
demonstration.
—*Author Unknown*

We need to find God and God cannot
be found in noise and restlessness.
—*Mother Teresa*

Bridle your anger, trash your
wrath, cool your pipes—it only
makes things worse.
—*King David, Psalms 37:8*

I slept and dreamt that life was joy.
I awoke and saw that life was service.
I acted and behold, service was joy.
—*Rabindranath Tagore*

Let there be peace on earth
and let it begin with me.
—*Barbara King*

If you want a picture of success as
heaven measures it, of greatness as God
view it, don't look for the blaring bands
of Broadway; listen, rather, for the tinkle
of water splashing into a basin, while
Christ, in humility that makes angels
hold their breath, sponges the grime
from the feet of his undeserving disciples.
—*Paul Rees*

Blessed is the influence of one true,
loving, human soul on another.
—*George Eliot*

If we take care of the moments, the
years will take care of themselves.
—*Maria Edgeworth*

To have and not to give is
often worse than to steal.
—*Marie von Ebner-Escenbach*

Never follow the crowd.
—*Bernard M. Baruch*

Do the duty which lies nearest to
you, the second duty will then
become clearer.
—*Thomas Carlyle*

We don't get to know people
when they come to us; we must
go to them to find out what
they are like.
—*Johann Wolfgang von Goethe*

Never, for the sake of peace and quiet,
deny your own experience or
convictions.
—*Dag Hammarskjöld*

God waits for the chances we give him
to show his great generosity.
—*Saint John Chrysostom, Fourth Century*

Nothing is stronger than habit.
—*Ovid*

I shall pass through this world but once.
If, therefore, there be any kindness
I can show, or any good thing I can do,
let me do it now, for I may never
pass this way again.
—From *The Magnificent Obsession*

Every painful event contains in itself a seed of growth and liberation.
—*Anthony de Mello*

I have learned that no matter how good a friend is, they're going to hurt you every once in a while and you must forgive them for that.
—*James Rhinehart*

Find a need and fill it.
—*Ruth Stafford Peale*

———— ✳ ————

To "let go" does not mean to
stop caring. It means I can't do it for
someone else. To "let go" is to admit
powerlessness, which means the outcome is not in my hands. To "let go" is
not to try to change or blame another.
It's to make the most of myself. To "let
go" is not to fix, but to be supportive.
To "let go" is not to judge but to allow
another to be a human being. To
"let go" is not to be in the middle,
arranging all the outcomes, but to allow
others to affect their own destinies.
—*Author Unknown*

Don't ever take a fence down until you
know why it was put up.
—*Robert Frost*

Happiness comes from spiritual wealth, not material wealth. . . . Happiness comes from giving, not getting. If we try hard to bring happiness to others, we cannot stop it from coming to us also. To get joy, we must give it, and to keep joy we must scatter it.
—*John Templeton*

There ain't no use trying to talk to God when you ain't speakin' to your neighbor.
—*Hambone Cartoon*

The future belongs to those who see
possibilities before they become obvious.
—*Author Unknown*

Love all the people you can.
The sufferings from love are not to be
compared to the sorrows of loneliness.
—*Susan Hale*

God is most glorified in us when we
are most satisfied in Him.
—*John Piper*

Money is a very excellent servant,
but a terrible master.
—*P. T. Barnum*

337

God has a history of using the
insignificant to accomplish
the impossible.
—*Richard Exley*

We are what we repeatedly do.
Excellence, then, is not an act
but a habit.
—*Aristotle*

If you expect another person
to make you happy, you'll be
endlessly disappointed.
—*M. Scott Peck*

Order your soul; reduce your wants;
live in charity; associate in Christian
community; obey the laws;
trust in Providence.

—*Saint Augustine*

Autobiography in Five Chapters:

CHAPTER ONE

I walk down the street. There is a deep
hole in the sidewalk. I fall in. I am lost. . .
I am hopeless. It isn't my fault. It takes
forever to find a way out.

CHAPTER TWO

I walk down the same street.
There is a deep hole in the sidewalk.
I pretend I don't see it. I fall in again.
I can't believe I'm in the same place.
But it isn't my fault. It still takes
a long time to get out.

CHAPTER THREE

I walk down the same street. There is a
deep hole in the sidewalk. I see it is
there. I still fall in . . . it's a habit. My
eyes are open. I know where I am. It is
my fault. I get out immediately.

CHAPTER FOUR

I walk down the same street. There is a
deep hole in the sidewalk. I walk
around it.

CHAPTER FIVE

I walk down another street.

—*Author Unknown*

Consider the source.
—*Ancient Proverb*

I am not more than a wisp of
smoke to the world, but to God I
am a flame of hope and promise
in a darkened room.
—*Joan Noeldechen*

It may be that when we no longer
know what to do, we have come to our
real work, and when we no longer
know which way to go, we have
begun our real journey.
—*Wendell Berry*

If you have a fault to find with anyone,
tell him, not others . . . There is no
more dangerous experiment than that
of undertaking to be one thing before a
man's face and another behind his back.
—*Robert E. Lee*

What we desire our children
to become, we must endeavor
to be before them.
—*Andrew Combe*

Make sure that you let them know that
you love them while you still
have many years to go.
—*Mason Ovian*

No man need stay the way he is.
—*Harry Emerson Fosdick*

Whatever your labors and aspirations,
in the noisy confusion of life
keep peace with your soul.
—*Max Ehrmann*

A word of encouragement during
a failure is worth more than an hour
of praise after success.
—*Author Unknown*

Forgiving those who hurt us
is the key to personal peace.
—*G. Weatherley*

Don't procrastinate. Putting off an
unpleasant task until tomorrow simply
gives you more time for your
imagination to make a mountain
out of a possible molehill.
—*Author Unknown*

Christ has no body now on earth
but yours;
Yours are the only hands with which he
can do his work,
Yours are the only feet with which he
can go about the world,
Yours are the only eyes through which
his compassion
Can shine forth upon a troubled world.
Christ has no body on earth now
but yours.
—*Mother Teresa*

The law of influence is that we
become like those we habitually admire.
—*Henry Drummond*

Just do what you do best.
—*Red Auerbach*

No day should be lived unless it was begun with a prayer of thankfulness and an intercession for guidance.
—*Robert E. Lee*

People do not care how much you know, till they know how much you care.
—*Brett Watson*

If you do not conquer self,
you will be conquered by self.
—*Napoleon Hill*

Every increased possession loads us
with new weariness.
—*John Ruskin*

Making a space in life for God and
prayer radically changes the whole of
that life, if it is lived out seriously.
—*Michael Hollings*

Be kind to unkind people;
they probably need it the most.
—*Ashleigh Brilliant*

Fools have short fuses and explode
all too quickly;
the prudent quietly shrug off insults.
—*King Solomon, Proverbs 12:16*

The least I can do is speak out for
those who cannot speak for themselves.
—*Jane Goodall*

Lower your expectations of earth. This isn't heaven, so don't expect it to be.
—*Max Lucado*

Do the next thing.
—*Author Unknown*

If at first you don't succeed, destroy
all evidence that you tried.
—*Author Unknown*

Begin again just where you are.
—*E. Glenn Hinson*

Don't concern yourself with things
you can't do anything about anyway.
Armchair generals don't win battles, but
they do have nervous breakdowns.
—*Author Unknown*

In my end, is my beginning.
—*Mary, Queen of Scots*

It is a very hard undertaking to seek
to please everybody.

—*Pliny*

Anger manages everything badly.

—*Statius*

You can't test courage cautiously.
—*Annie Dillard*

Things are not always what they seem.
—*Phaedrus*

We are more likely to catch glimpses
of truth when we allow what we think
and believe to be tested.
—*Choan-Seng Song*

The art of the quoter is to
know when to stop.
—*Robertson Davies*